The Design of Future Things

The Design
of Future Things

Donald A. Norman

BASIC BOOKS

A MEMBER OF THE PERSEUS BOOKS GROUP

NEW YORK

Copyright © 2007 by Donald A. Norman
Published by Basic Books,
A Member of the Perseus Books Group

Books published by Basic Books are available at special discounts for bulk purchases in the United States by corporations, institutions, and other organizations. For more information, please contact the Special Markets Department at the Perseus Books Group, 2300 Chestnut Street, Suite 200, Philadelphia, PA 19103, or call (800) 255–1514, or e-mail special.markets@perseusbooks.com.

Designed by Timm Bryson
Set in 11.5 point Minion

Library of Congress Cataloging-in-Publication Data

Norman, Donald A.
  The design of future things / Donald A. Norman.
    p. cm.
  Includes bibliographical references and index.
  ISBN-13: 978-0-465-00227-6
  ISBN-10: 0-465-00227-7
  1. Design, Industrial—Psychological aspects. 2. Human engineering. I. Title.

TS171.4.N668 2007
745.2—dc22
                        2007035377

BOOKS BY DONALD A. NORMAN

Textbooks

Memory and Attention: An Introduction to Human Information Processing. (First edition, 1969; second edition 1976.)

Human Information Processing. (With Peter Lindsay: First edition, 1972; second edition 1977.)

Scientific Monographs

Models of Human Memory. (Edited, 1970.)

Explorations in Cognition. (With David E. Rumelhart and the LNR Research Group, 1975.)

Perspectives on Cognitive Science. (Edited, 1981.)

User Centered System Design: New Perspectives on Human-Computer Interaction. (Edited with Steve Draper, 1986.)

Trade Books

Learning and Memory, 1982.

The Psychology of Everyday Things, 1988.

The Design of Everyday Things, 1990 and 2002. (Paperback version of *The Psychology of Everyday Things.*)

Turn Signals Are the Facial Expressions of Automobiles, 1992.

Things That Make Us Smart, 1993.

The Invisible Computer: Why Good Products Can Fail, the Personal Computer Is So Complex, and Information Appliances Are the Solution, 1998

Emotional Design: Why We Love (or Hate) Everyday Things, 2004

CD-ROM

First Person: Donald A. Norman. Defending Human Attributes in the Age of the Machine, 1994.

Contents

CHAPTER ONE

Cautious Cars and Cantankerous Kitchens

How Machines Take Control

I'm driving my car through the winding mountain roads between my home and the Pacific Ocean. Sharp curves drop off steeply amidst the towering redwood trees and vistas of the San Francisco Bay on one side and the Pacific Ocean on the other. It's a wonderful drive, the car responding effortlessly to the challenge, negotiating sharp turns with grace. At least, that's how I am feeling. But then I notice that my wife is tense: she's scared. Her feet are braced against the floor, her shoulders hunched, her arms against the dashboard. "What's the matter?" I ask, "Calm down, I know what I'm doing."

Now imagine another scenario. I'm driving on the same winding, mountain road, and I notice that my car is tense: it's scared. The seats straighten, the seat belts tighten, and the dashboard starts beeping at me. I notice the brakes are being applied automatically. "Oops," I think, "I'd better slow down."

Do you think the idea of a frightened automobile fanciful? Let me assure you, it is not. This behavior already exists on some luxury automobiles—and more is being planned. Stray out of your lane, and some cars balk: beeping, perhaps vibrating the wheel or the seat or flashing lights in the side mirrors. Automobile companies are experimenting with partial correction, helping the driver steer the car back into its own lane. Turn signals were designed to tell other drivers that you are going to turn or switch lanes, but now they are how you tell your own car that you really do wish to turn or change lanes: "Hey, don't try to stop me," they say to your car. "I'm doing this on purpose."

I was once a member of a panel of consultants advising a major automobile manufacturer. I described how I would respond differently to my wife than my car. "How come?" asked fellow panelist Sherry Turkle, an MIT professor and an authority on the relationship between people and technology. "How come you listen to your car more than your wife?"

How come, indeed. Sure, I can make up rational explanations, but they will miss the point. As we start giving the objects around us more initiative, more intelligence, and more emotion and personality, we now have to worry about how we interact with our machines.

Why do I appear to pay more attention to my car than to my wife? The answer is complex, but in the end, it comes down to communication. When my wife complains, I can ask her why, then either agree with her or try to reassure her. I can also modify my driving so that she is not so disturbed by it. But I can't have a conversation with my car: all the communication is one way.

"Do you like your new car?" I asked Tom, who was driving me to the airport after a lengthy meeting. "How do you like the navigation system?"

> "I love the car," said Tom, "but I never use the naviga-
> tion system. I don't like it: I like to decide what route I will
> take. It doesn't give me any say."

Machines have less power than humans, so they have more authority. Contradictory? Yes, but, oh, so true. Consider who has more power in a business negotiation. If you want to make the strongest possible deal, who should you send to the bargaining table, the CEO or someone at a lower level? The answer is counterintuitive: quite often, the lower-level employee can make the better deal. Why? Because no matter how powerful the opposing arguments, the weak representative cannot close the deal. Even in the face of persuasive arguments, he or she can only say, "I'm sorry, but I can't give you an answer until I consult with my boss," only to come back the next day and say, "I'm sorry, but I couldn't convince my boss." A powerful negotiator, on the other hand, might be convinced and accept the offer, even if later, there was regret.

Successful negotiators understand this bargaining ploy and won't let their opponents get away with it. When I discussed this with a friend, a successful lawyer, she laughed at me. "Hey," she said, "if the other side tried that on me, I'd call them on it. I won't let them play that game with me." Machines do play this game on us, and we don't have any way of refusing. When the machine intervenes, we have no alternatives except to let it take over: "It's this or nothing," they are saying, where "nothing" is not an option.

Consider Tom's predicament. He asks his car's navigation system for directions, and it provides them. Sounds simple.

Human-machine interaction: a nice dialogue. But notice Tom's lament: "It doesn't give me any say." Designers of advanced technology are proud of the "communication capabilities" they have built into their systems. But closer analysis shows this to be a misnomer: there is no communication, none of the back-and-forth discussion that characterizes true dialogue. Instead, we have two monologues. We issue commands to the machine, and it, in turn, commands us. Two monologues do not make a dialogue.

In this particular case, Tom does have a choice. If he turns the navigation system off, the car still functions, so because his navigation system doesn't give him enough say over the route, he simply doesn't use it. But other systems do not provide this option: the only way to avoid them is not to use the car. The problem is that these systems can be of great value. Flawed though they may be, they can save lives. The question, then, is how we can change the way we interact with our machines to take better advantage of their strengths and virtues, while at the same time eliminating their annoying and sometimes dangerous actions.

As our technology becomes more powerful, its failure in terms of collaboration and communication becomes ever more critical. Collaboration means synchronizing one's activities, as well as explaining and giving reasons. It means having trust, which can only be formed through experience and understanding. With automatic, so-called intelligent devices, trust is sometimes conferred undeservedly—or withheld, equally undeservedly. Tom decided not to trust his navigational system's instructions, but in some instances, rejecting technology can cause harm. For example, what if Tom turned off his car's antiskid brakes or the stability control? Many drivers believe they can control the car better than these automatic controls. But antiskid and stability systems actually perform far better than all but the most expert professional drivers. They have saved many lives. But how does the driver know which systems can be trusted?

Designers tend to focus on the technology, attempting to automate whatever possible for safety and convenience. Their goal is complete automation, except where this is not yet possible because of technical limitations or cost concerns. These limitations, however, mean that the tasks can only be partially automated, so the person must always monitor the action and take over whenever the machine can no longer perform properly. Whenever a task is only partially automated, it is essential that each party, human and machine, know what the other is doing and what is intended.

Two Monologues Do Not Make a Dialogue

> SOCRATES: You know, Phaedrus, that's the strange thing about writing. . . . they seem to talk to you as if they were intelligent, but if you ask them anything about what they say, from a desire to be instructed, they go on telling you just the same thing forever.
>
> —Plato: Collected Dialogues, 1961.

Two thousand years ago, Socrates argued that the book would destroy people's ability to reason. He believed in dialogue, in conversation and debate. But with a book, there is no debate: the written word cannot answer back. Today, the book is such a symbol of learning and knowledge that we laugh at this argument. But take it seriously for a moment. Despite Socrates's claims, writing does instruct because we do not need to debate its content with the author. Instead, we debate and discuss with one another, in the classroom, with discussion groups, and if the work is important enough, through all the media at our disposal. Nonetheless, Socrates's point is valid: a technology that gives no opportunity for discussion, explanation, or debate is a poor technology.

As a business executive and as a chair of university departments, I learned that the process of making a decision is often more important than the decision itself. When a person makes decisions without explanation or consultation, people neither trust nor like the result, even if it is the identical course of action they would have taken after discussion and debate. Many business leaders ask, "Why waste time with meetings when the end result will be the same?" But the end result is not the same, for although the decision itself is identical, the way it will be carried out and executed and, perhaps most importantly, the way it will be handled if things do not go as planned will be very different with a collaborating, understanding team than with one that is just following orders.

Tom dislikes his navigation system, even though he agrees that at times it would be useful. But he has no way to interact with the system to tailor it to his needs. Even if he can make some high-level choices—"fastest," "shortest," "most scenic," or "avoid toll road"—he can't discuss with the system why a particular route is chosen. He can't know why the system thinks route A is better than route B. Does it take into account the long traffic signals and the large number of stop signs? And what if two routes barely differ, perhaps by just a minute out of an hour's journey? He isn't given alternatives that he might well prefer despite a slight cost in time. The system's methods remain hidden so that even if Tom were tempted to trust it, the silence and secrecy promotes distrust, just as top-down business decisions made without collaboration are distrusted.

What if navigation systems were able to discuss the route with the driver? What if they presented alternative routes, displaying them both as paths on a map and as a table showing the distance, estimated driving time, and cost, allowing the driver to choose? Some navigation systems do this, so that the drive from a city in California's Napa Valley to Palo Alto might be presented like this:

FROM ST. HELENA, CA TO PALO ALTO, CA

	DISTANCE	ESTIMATED TIME	ROUTE	TOLLS
1	94.5 Miles	1 Hour 46 Minutes	Via Dumbarton Bridge	$4
2	98.3 Miles	1 Hour 50 Minutes	Via San Francisco Bay Bridge	$4
3	103.6 Miles	2 Hours 10 Minutes	Via Golden Gate Bridge	$5

This is a clear improvement, but it still isn't a conversation. The system says, "Here are three choices: select one." I can't ask for details or seek some modification. I am familiar with all these routes, so I happen to know that the fastest, shortest, cheapest route is also the least scenic, and the most scenic route is not even offered. But what about the driver who is not so knowledgeable? We would never settle for such limited engagement with a human driver. The fact that navigation systems offering drivers even this limited choice of routes are considered a huge improvement over existing systems demonstrates how bad the others are, how far we still have to go.

If my car decides an accident is imminent and straightens the seat or applies the brakes, I am not asked or consulted; nor am I even told why. Is the car necessarily more accurate because, after all, it is a mechanical, electronic technology that does precise arithmetic without error? No, actually it's not. The arithmetic may be correct, but before doing the computation, it must make assumptions about the road, the other traffic, and the capabilities of the driver. Professional drivers will sometimes turn off automatic equipment because they know the automation will not allow them to deploy their skills. That is, they will turn off whatever they are permitted to turn off: many modern cars are so authoritarian that they do not even allow this choice.

Don't think that these behaviors are restricted to the automobile. The devices of the future will present the same issues in a wide variety of settings. Automatic banking systems already exist that determine whether you are eligible for a loan. Automated medical systems determine whether you should receive a particular treatment or medication. Future systems will monitor your eating, your reading, your music and television preferences. Some systems will watch where you drive, alerting the insurance company, the rental car agency, or even the police if they decide that you have violated their rules. Other systems monitor for copyright violations, making decisions about what should be permitted. In all these cases, actions are apt to be taken arbitrarily, with the systems making gross assumptions about your intentions from a limited sample of your behavior.

So-called intelligent systems have become too smug. They think they know what is best for us. Their intelligence, however, is limited. And this limitation is fundamental: there is no way a machine has sufficient knowledge of all the factors that go into human decision making. But this doesn't mean we should reject the assistance of intelligent machines. As machines start to take over more and more, however, they need to be socialized; they need to improve the way they communicate and interact and to recognize their limitations. Only then can they become truly useful. This is a major theme of this book.

When I started writing this book, I thought that the key to socializing machines was to develop better systems for dialogue. But I was wrong. Successful dialogue requires shared knowledge and experiences. It requires appreciation of the environment and context, of the history leading up to the moment, and of the many differing goals and motives of the people involved. I now believe this to be a fundamental limitation of today's technology, one that prevents machines from full, humanlike interaction. It is hard enough to establish this shared, common understanding with people, so how do we expect to be able to develop it with machines?

In order to cooperate usefully with our machines, we need to regard the interaction somewhat as we do interaction with animals. Although both humans and animals are intelligent, we are different species, with different understandings and different capabilities. Similarly, even the most intelligent machine is a different species, with its own set of strengths and weaknesses, its own set of understandings and capabilities. Sometimes we need to obey the animals or machines; sometimes they need to obey us.

Where Are We Going? Who Is in Charge?

"My car almost got me into an accident," Jim told me.

"Your car? How could that be?" I asked.

"I was driving down the highway using the adaptive cruise control. You know, the control that keeps my car at a constant speed unless there is a car in front, and then it slows up to keep a safe distance. Well, after awhile, the road got crowded, so my car slowed. Eventually, I came to my exit, so I maneuvered into the right lane and then turned off the highway. By then, I had been using the cruise control for so long, but going so slowly, that I had forgotten about it. But not the car. I guess it said to itself, 'Hurrah! Finally, there's no one in front of me,' and it started to accelerate to full highway speed, even though this was the off-ramp that requires a slow speed. Good thing I was alert and stepped on the brakes in time. Who knows what might have happened."

We are in the midst of a major change in how we relate to technology. Until recently, people have been in control. We turned the technology on and off, told it which operation to perform, and guided it through its operations. As technology became more powerful and complex, we became less able to understand how it worked, less able to predict its actions. Once computers and microprocessors entered the scene, we often found ourselves lost and confused, annoyed and angered. But still, we considered ourselves to be in control. No longer. Now, our machines are taking over. They act as if they have intelligence and volition, even though they don't.

Machines monitor us with the best of intentions, of course, in the interest of safety, convenience, or accuracy. When everything works, these smart machines can indeed be helpful, increasing safety, reducing the boredom of tedious tasks, making our lives more convenient, and performing tasks more accurately than we could. It is indeed convenient that the automobile automatically slows when a car darts too closely in front of us, that it shifts gears quietly and smoothly, or, in the home, that our microwave oven knows just when the potatoes are cooked. But what about when the technology fails? What about when it does the wrong thing or fights with us for control? What about when Jim's auto notices that there are no cars in front of it, so it accelerates to highway speed, even though it is no longer on a highway? The same mechanisms that are so helpful when things are normal can decrease safety, decrease comfort, and decrease accuracy when unexpected situations arise. For us, the people involved, it leads to danger and discomfort, frustration and anger.

Today, machines primarily signal their states through alerts and alarms, meaning only when they get into trouble. When a machine fails, a person is required to take over, often with no advance warning and often with insufficient time to react properly. Jim was able to correct his car's behavior in time, but what if he couldn't have? He would have been blamed for causing an accident. Ironically, if the actions of a so-called intelligent device lead to an accident, it will probably be blamed on human error!

The proper way to provide for smooth interaction between people and intelligent devices is to enhance the coordination and cooperation of both parties, people and machines. But those who design these systems often don't understand this. How is a machine to judge what is or is not important, especially when what is important in one situation may not be in another?

I have told the story of Jim and his enthusiastic car to engineers from several automobile companies. Their responses always have two components. First, they blame the driver. Why didn't he turn off the cruise control before exiting? I explain that he had forgotten about it. Then he was a poor driver, is their response. This kind of "blame-and-train" philosophy always makes the blamer, the insurance company, the legislative body, or society feel good: if people make errors, punish them. But it doesn't solve the underlying problem. Poor design, and often poor procedures, poor infrastructure, and poor operating practices, are the true culprits: people are simply the last step in this complex process.

Although the car companies are technically correct that the driver should remember the mode of the car's automation, that is no excuse for poor design. We must design our technologies for the way people actually behave, not the way we would like them to behave. Moreover, the automobile does not help the driver remember. In fact, it seems more designed to help the driver forget! There is hardly any clue as to the state of the cruise control system: the car could do a far better job of reminding the driver of what control it has assumed.

When I say this to engineers, they promptly introduce the second component of their response: "Yes, this is a problem, but don't worry. We will fix it. You're right; the car's navigation system should realize that the car is now on the exit road, so it should automatically either disconnect the cruise control or, at least, change its setting to a safe speed."

This illustrates the fundamental problem. The machine is not intelligent: the intelligence is in the mind of the designer. Designers sit in their offices, attempting to imagine all that might happen to the car and driver, and then devise solutions. But how can the designers determine the appropriate response to something unexpected? When this happens to a person, we can expect creative, imaginative problem solving. Because the "intelligence" in our machines is not in the device but in the heads of the designers so when the unexpected happens, the designer isn't there to help out, so the machine usually fails.

We know two things about unexpected events: first, they always occur, and second, when they do occur, they are always unexpected.

I once got a third response from an automobile company engineer about Jim's experience. He sheepishly admitted that the exit lane problem had happened to him, but that there was yet another problem: lane changing. On a busy highway, if a driver decides to change lanes, he or she waits until there is a sufficiently large gap in the traffic in the new lane, then quickly darts over. That usually means that the car is close to those in front and behind. The adaptive cruise control is likely to decide the car is too close to the car in front and therefore brake.

"What's the problem with that?" I asked. "Yes, it's annoying, but it sounds safe to me."

"No," said the engineer. "It's dangerous because the driver in back of you didn't expect you to dart in and then suddenly put on the brakes. If they aren't paying close attention, they could run into you from behind. But even if they don't hit you, the driver behind is annoyed with your driving behavior."

"Maybe," said the engineer, laughing, "the car should have a special brake light that comes on when the brakes are applied by the automobile itself rather than by the driver, telling the car behind, 'Hey, don't blame me. The car did it.'"

The engineer was joking, but his comments reveal the tensions between the behavior of people and machines. People take actions for all sorts of reasons, some good, some bad, some considerate, some reckless. Machines are more consistent, evaluating the situation according to the logic and rules programmed into them. But machines have fundamental limitations: they do not sense the world in the same way as people, they lack higher order goals, and they have no way of understanding the goals and motives of the people with whom they must interact. Machines, in other words, are fundamentally different: superior in some ways, especially in speed, power, and consistency, inferior in others, especially in social skills, creativity, and imagination. Machines lack the empathy required to consider how their actions impact those around them. These differences, especially in what we would call social skills and empathy, are the cause of the problems. Moreover, these differences—and therefore these conflicts—are fundamental, not ones that can be quickly fixed by changing the logic here or adding a new sensor there.

As a result, the actions of machines contradict what people would do. In many cases, this is perfectly fine: if my washing machine cleans clothes very differently than I would, I don't care as long as the end result is clean clothes. Machine automation works here because once the washing machine has been loaded and started, it is a closed environment. Once started, the machine takes over, and as long as I refrain from interfering, everything works smoothly.

But what about environments where both people and machines work together? Or what happens with my washing machine if I change my mind after it has started? How do I tell it to use different setting, and once the washing cycle has started, when will the changes take effect—right away or with the next filling of the machine? Here, the differences between the way machines and people react really matter. Sometimes, it appears that the machine is acting completely arbitrarily, although if the machine could think and talk, I suspect it would explain that from its point of view, the person is the one being arbitrary. To the person, this can be frustrating, a continual battle of wills. To the observer, it can be confusing, for it is never clear who is in charge or why a particular action has been taken. It doesn't really matter whether the machine or the person is correct: it is the mismatch that matters, for this is what gives rise to aggravation, frustration, and, in some cases, damage or injury.

The conflict between human and machine actions is fundamental because machines, whatever their capabilities, simply do not know enough about the environment, the goals and motives of the people, and the special circumstances that invariably surround any set of activities. Machines work very well when they work in controlled environments, where no pesky humans get in the way, where there are no unexpected events, and where everything can be predicted with great accuracy. That's where automation shines.

But even though the machines work well when they have complete control of the environment, even here they don't quite do things the way we would. Consider the "smart" microwave. It knows just how much power to apply and how long to cook. When it works, it is very nice: you simply have to put in fresh salmon and tell the machine you are cooking fish. Out it comes, cooked to perfection, somewhere between a poached fish and a steamed one, but perfect in its own way. "The Sensor features detect the increasing humidity released during cooking," says the manual, "[and] the oven automatically adjusts the cooking time to various types and amounts of food." But notice that it doesn't determine if the microwave cooks the food in the same way that a person would. A person would test the firmness, look at the color, or perhaps measure the internal temperature. The microwave oven can't do any of this, so it measures what it can: the humidity. It uses the humidity to infer the cooking level. For fish and vegetables, this seems to work fine, but not for everything. Moreover, the sensing technology is not perfect. If the food comes out undercooked, the manual warns against using the sensor a second time: "Do not use the Sensor features twice in succession on the same food portion—it may result in severely overcooked or burnt food." So much for the intelligent microwave.

Do these machines aid the home dweller? Yes and no. If machines can be said to have a "voice," theirs is certainly condescending, offering no hint as to how or why they do what they do, no hint as to what they are doing, no hint as to the amount of doneness, cleanliness, or drying the machine is inferring from its sensing, and no idea of what to do when things don't work properly. Many people, quite appropriately in my opinion, shun these devices. "Why is it doing this?" interested parties want to know. There is no word from the machines and hardly a word from the manuals.

In research laboratories around the world, scientists are working on even more ways of introducing machine intelligence into our lives. There are experimental homes that sense all the actions of their inhabitants, turning the lights on and off, adjusting the room temperature, even selecting the music. The list of projects in the works is impressive: refrigerators that refuse to let you eat inappropriate foods, tattletale toilets that secretly tell your physician about the state of your body fluids. Refrigerators and toilets may seem an unlikely pairing, but they team up to monitor eating behavior, the one attempting to control what goes into the body, the other measuring and assessing what comes out. We have scolding scales watching over weight. Exercise machines demanding to be used. Even teapots shrilly whistling at us, demanding immediate attention.

As we add more and more smart devices to daily life, our lives are transformed both for good and for bad. This is good when the devices work as promised—and bad when they fail or when they transform productive, creative people into servants continually looking after their machines, getting them out of trouble, repairing them, and maintaining them. This is not the way it was supposed to be, but it certainly is the way it is. Is it too late? Can we do something about it?

The Rise of the Smart Machine
Toward a Natural, Symbiotic Relationship

The hope is that in not too many years, human brains and computing machines will be coupled together very tightly,

and that the resulting partnership will think as no human
brain has ever thought.

—J. C. R. Licklider, "Man-Computer Symbiosis," 1960.

In the 1950s, the psychologist J. C. R. Licklider attempted to determine how people and machines could interact gracefully and harmoniously, or in what he called a "symbiotic relationship," so that the resulting partnership would enhance our lives. What would it mean to have a graceful symbiosis of people and technology? We need a more natural form of interaction, an interaction that can take place subconsciously, without effort, whereby the communication in both directions is done so naturally, so effortlessly, that the result is a smooth merger of person and machine, jointly performing a task.

There are numerous instances of "natural interaction." Let me discuss four that demonstrate different kinds of relations: between people and traditional tools, between horse and rider, between driver and automobile, and one involving machine automation, "recommendation" systems that suggest books to read, music to listen to, and films to watch.

Skilled artisans work their materials through their tools, just as musicians relate with their instruments. Whether used by a painter or sculptor, woodworker or musician, their tools and instruments feel like a part of the body. So, craftspeople do not act as if they are using tools but as if they are directly manipulating the items of interest: paint on canvas, sculptured material, wood, or musical sounds. The feel of the materials provides feedback to the person: smooth and resonant here, bumpy or rough there. The interaction is complex but pleasurable. This symbiotic relationship only occurs when the person is well skilled and the tools are well designed. When it happens, this interaction is positive, pleasurable, and effective.

Think of skilled horseback riders. The rider "reads" the horse, just as the horse can read its rider. Each conveys information to the other about what is ahead. Horses communicate with their riders through body language, gait, readiness to proceed, and their general behavior: wary, skittish, and edgy or eager, lively, and playful. In turn, riders communicate with horses through their body language, the way they sit, the pressures exerted by their knees, feet, and heels, and the signals they communicate with their hands and reins. Riders also communicate ease and mastery or discomfort and unease. This interaction is positive example two. It is of special interest because it is an example of two sentient systems, horse and rider, both intelligent, both interpreting the world and communicating their interpretations to each other.

Example three is similar to the horse and rider, except that now we have a sentient being interacting with a sophisticated, but nonsentient, machine. At its best this is a graceful interaction between the feel of the automobile, the track, and the actions of the driver.

I think of this when I sit beside my son while he drives my highly tuned German sports car at high speed on the racetrack that we have rented for the afternoon. We approach a sharp curve, and I watch as he gently brakes, shifting the car's weight forward, then turns the steering wheel so that as the front end of the car turns, the rear end, now with reduced weight bearing down, skids, putting the car into a deliberate, controlled skid, known as an "oversteer" condition. As the rear end swings

around, my son straightens the steering wheel and accelerates, shifting the car's weight back to the rear wheels so that we are once again accelerating smoothly down a straightaway with the pleasure of feeling in complete control. All three of us have enjoyed the experience: me, my son, and the car.

Example four, the recommendation system, is very different from the other three for it is slower, less graceful, and more intellectual. Nonetheless, it is an excellent example of a positive interaction between people and complex systems, primarily because it suggests without controlling, without annoyance: we are free to accept or ignore its recommendations. These systems work in a variety of ways, but all suggest items or activities that you might like by analyzing your past selections or activities, searching for similarities to other items in their databases, and by examining the likes and dislikes of other people whose interests appear similar to yours. As long as the recommendations are presented in a noninvasive fashion, eliciting your voluntary examination and participation, they can be helpful. Consider the search for a book on one of the internet websites. Being able to read an excerpt and examine the table of contents, index, and reviews helps us decide whether to make a purchase.

Some sites even explain why they have made their recommendations, offering to let people tune their preference settings. I have seen recommendation systems in research laboratories that watch over your activities, so if you are reading or writing, they suggest articles to read by finding items that are similar in content to what is on your display. These systems work well for several reasons. First, they do offer value, for the suggestions are often relevant and useful. Second, they are presented in a nonintrusive manner, off to the side, without distracting you from the primary task but readily available when you are ready. Not all recommendation systems are so effective, for some are intrusive—some seem to violate one's privacy. When done well, they demonstrate that intelligent systems can add pleasure and value to our interactions with machines.

A Caveat

When I ride a horse, it isn't any fun for me or the horse. Smooth, graceful interaction between horse and rider requires considerable skill, which I lack. I don't know what I am doing, and both I and the horse know this. Similarly, I watch drivers who are neither skilled nor confident struggle with their automobiles, and I, as a passenger, do not feel safe. Symbiosis is a wonderful concept, a cooperative, beneficial relationship. But in some cases, as in my first three examples, it requires considerable effort, training, and skill. In other cases, such as in my fourth example, although no high-level skill or training is required, the designers of these systems must pay careful attention to appropriate modes of social interaction.

After I had posted a draft version of this chapter on my website, I received a letter from a group of researchers who were exploring the metaphor of horse and rider to the control of automobiles and airplanes. The "H-metaphor," they called it, where "H" stands for "horse." Scientists at the American National Aeronautics and Space Administration research facilities at Langley, Virginia, were collaborating with scientists at the German Aerospace Center's Institute for Transportation Systems in Braunschweig, Germany, to understand just how such systems might be built. I visited Braunschweig to learn more about their work (fascinating stuff, to which I return in chapter 3). Riders, it seems, delegate the amount of control they give to the horse: when using "loose reins," the horse has authority, but under "tight reins," the rider exerts more control. Skilled riders are in continual negotiation with their horses, adjusting the amount of control they maintain to the circumstances. The American and German scientists are trying to replicate this relationship with human-machine interaction—not only with cars but with houses and appliances.

Symbiosis, in the sense meant by Licklider half a century ago, is a merger of two components, one human, one machine, where the mix is smooth and fruitful, the resulting collaboration exceeding what either is capable of alone. We need to understand how best to accomplish this interaction, how to make it so natural that training and skill are usually not required.

Skittish Horses, Skittish Machines

What would it mean for a car and driver to interact much as a skilled rider interacts with a horse? Suppose a car were to balk or act skittish when getting too close to the cars ahead or when driving at a speed it computed to be dangerous? Suppose the car responded smoothly and gracefully to appropriate commands and sluggishly and reluctantly to others? Would it be possible to devise a car whose physical responsiveness communicated the safety status to the driver?

What about your house? What would it mean to have a skittish house? I can see my vacuum cleaner or stove acting up, wanting to do one thing when I wanted it to do another. But my house? Today companies are poised to transform your home into an automated beast, always looking out for your best interests, providing you with everything you need and desire, even before you know you need or desire it. Many companies are anxious to equip, wire, and control these "smart homes"— homes that control the lighting according to their perception of your moods, that choose what music to play or that direct the television images to move from screen to screen as you wander about the house. All these "smart" and "intelligent" devices pose the question of how we will be able to relate to all this smartness. If we want to learn to ride a horse, we have to practice or, better yet, take lessons. So, do we need to practice how to use our home, to take lessons on getting along with our appliances?

What if we could devise natural means of interaction between people and machines? Could we learn from the way that skilled riders interact with horses? Perhaps. We would need to determine the appropriate behavioral mappings between the behaviors and states of the horse and rider and those of the car and driver. How would a car indicate nervousness? What is the equivalent for a car to a horse's posture or skittishness? If a horse conveys its emotional state by rearing back and tensing its neck, what might the equivalent be for a car? What if suddenly your car reared back, lowering its rear end while raising the front, perhaps moving the front end left and right?

Natural signals akin to what the horse receives from its rider are actually being explored in research laboratories. Research scientists in the automobile companies are experimenting with measures of emotion and attention, and at least one automobile model sold to the public does have a television camera located on the steering column that watches drivers, deciding whether or not they are paying attention. If the automobile decides that a crash is imminent but the driver is looking elsewhere, it brakes.

Similarly, scientists are hard at work developing smart homes that monitor the inhabitants, assessing their moods and emotions, and adjusting room temperature, lighting, and background music. I've visited several of these experiments and observed the results. At one research facility at a European university, people were asked to play a stressful video game, then allowed to rest afterwards in a special experimental room equipped with comfortable chairs, friendly and aesthetically pleasing furniture, and specially equipped lighting designed to relax the inhabitants. When I tried it, I found it to be a calm and restful environment. The goal of the research was to understand how to develop room environments appropriate to a person's emotional state. Could a home relax its inhabitants automatically when it detected stress? Or perhaps the home could take on a zingy, upbeat mood with bright lights, lively music, and warm colors when it determined that the inhabitants needed an energy boost.

Thinking for Machines Is Easy; Physical Actions Are Hard; Logic Is Simple, Emotion Difficult

"Follow me," says Manfred Macx, the hero/narrator of Charles Stross's science fiction novel *Accelerando,* to his newly purchased luggage. And follow him it does, "his new luggage rolling at his heels" as he turns and walks away.

Many of us grew up with the robots and giant brains of novels, movies, and television, where machines were all-powerful, sometimes clumsy (think of *Star Wars'* C–3PO), sometimes omniscient (think of *2001's* HAL), and sometimes indistinguishable from people (think of Rick Deckard, hero of the movie *Blade Runner*: is he human or replicant?). Reality is rather different from fiction: twenty-first century robots can't conduct any meaningful communication with people; indeed, they are barely capable of walking, and their ability to manipulate real objects in the world is pathetically weak. As a result, most intelligent devices—especially in the home, where costs must be kept down and reliability and ease of use kept up—concentrate on mundane tasks such as making coffee, washing clothes and dishes, controlling lights, heating, and air conditioning, and vacuuming, mopping, and cutting the grass.

If the task is very well specified and the environment under control, then intelligent machines can indeed do a reasonable, informed job. They can sense temperature and moisture, as well as the amount of liquid, clothing, or food, and thus determine when the laundry is dry or the food is cooked. The latest models of washing machines can even figure out what kind of material is being washed, how large the load is, and how dirty the clothes are, and adjust itself accordingly.

Vacuum cleaners and mops work as long as the pathway is relatively smooth and clear of obstacles, but the luggage that follows its owner in Stross's *Accelerando* is still beyond the capability of affordable machines. Nonetheless, though, this is precisely what a machine might be able to do, for it doesn't require real interaction with people: no communication, no safety-related issues, just follow along. What if someone tried to steal the freewheeling suitcase? It could be programmed to scream loudly at any attempt, and Stross tells us that it has learned the owner's "fingerprints, digital and phenotypic": thieves might be able to steal it, but they wouldn't be able to open it.

But could the luggage really make its way through crowded streets? People have feet, the better to step over and around obstacles, to go up and down stairs and over curbs. The luggage, with its wheels, would behave like a handicapped object, so it would need to seek out curb cuts at street intersections and ramps and elevators to maneuver within buildings. Human wheelchair users are often stymied: the wheeled luggage would be even more frustrated. And beyond curbs and stairs, navigating through city traffic would likely defeat its visual processing systems. Its ability to track its owner, avoid obstacles, and find paths navigable by a nonlegged device, while avoiding collisions with automobiles, bicycles, and people, would surely be compromised.

There is an interesting disjunction between the things people and machines find easy and hard. Thinking, which once was held up as the pinnacle of human achievement, is the area in which machines have made the greatest progress, especially any thinking that requires logic and attention to detail. Physical actions, such as standing, walking, jumping, and avoiding obstacles, are relatively easy for people, but difficult if not impossible for machines. Emotions play an essential role in human and animal behavior, helping us judge what is good or bad, safe or unsafe, while also providing a powerful communication system for conveying feelings and beliefs, reactions and intentions among people. Machine emotions are simplistic.

Despite these limitations many scientists are still striving to create the grand dream of intelligent machines that will communicate effectively with human beings. It is in the nature of research scientists to be optimists, to believe that they are doing the most important activity in the world and, moreover, that they are close to significant breakthroughs. The result is a plethora of news articles, such as this one:

> Researchers say robots soon will be able to perform many tasks for people, from child care to driving for the elderly.
>
> Some of the country's leading robotics experts gathered here Saturday at the annual meeting of the American Association for the Advancement of Science to present their latest research and talk about a future rife with robots. . . .
>
> [Y]our future could include: a huggable teddy bear that tutors your kids in Spanish or French; an autonomous car that drives you to work while you nap, eat or prepare your PowerPoint presentation; a Chihuahua-sized pet dinosaur that learns whether you like to cuddle, play or be left

alone; a computer that can move its screen to help your posture or match your task or mood; and a party-bot that greets your guests at the door, introduces them in case you've forgotten their names, and entertains them with music, jokes and finger food.

Many conferences are held to discuss progress on the development of "smart environments." Here is the wording of one invitation among the many that I receive:

> **Symposium on Affective Smart Environment. Newcastle Upon Tyne, UK.**
>
> Ambient Intelligence is an emerging and popular research field with the goal to create "smart" environments that react in an attentive, adaptive and proactive way to the presence and activities of humans, in order to provide the services that inhabitants of these environments request or are presumed to need.
>
> Ambient Intelligence is increasingly affecting our everyday lives: computers are already embedded in numerous everyday objects like TV sets, kitchen appliances, or central heating, and soon they will be networked, with each other. . . . [B]io-sensing will allow devices to perceive the presence and state of users and to understand their needs and goals in order to improve their general living conditions and actual well-being.

Do you trust your house to know what is best for you? Do you want the kitchen to talk to your bathroom scale, or perhaps to have your toilet run an automatic urinalysis, sharing the results with your medical clinic? And how, anyway, would the kitchen really know what you were eating? How would the kitchen know that the butter, eggs, and cream taken out of the refrigerator were for you, rather than for some other member of the household, or for a visitor, or maybe even for a school project?

Although monitoring eating habits wasn't really possible until recently, we can now attach tiny, barely visible tags on everything: clothes, products, food, items, even people and pets, so everything and everybody can be tracked. These are called radio frequency identification (RFID) tags. No batteries are required because these devices cleverly take their power from the very signal sent to them asking them to state their business, their identification number, and any other tidbits about the person or object they feel like sharing. When all the food in the house is tagged, the house knows what you are eating. RFID tags plus TV cameras, microphones, and other sensors equals "Eat your broccoli," "No more butter," "Do your exercises." Cantankerous kitchens? That's the least of it.

"What if appliances could understand what you need?" asked one group of researchers at the MIT Media Lab. They built a kitchen with sensors everywhere they could put them, television cameras, and pressure gauges on the floor to determine where people were standing. The system, they said, "infers that when a person uses the fridge and then stands in front of the microwave, he/she has a high probability of re-heating food." "KitchenSense," they call it. Here is their description:

> KitchenSense is a sensor-rich networked kitchen research
> platform that uses CommonSense reasoning to simplify
> control interfaces and augment interaction. The system's

sensor net attempts to interpret people's intentions to create fail-soft support for safe, efficient and aesthetic activity.
By considering embedded sensor data together with daily-
event knowledge, a centrally-controlled OpenMind system
can develop a shared context across various appliances.

If people use the refrigerator and then walk to the microwave
oven, they have a "high probability of reheating food." This is
highfalutin scientific jargon for guessing. Oh, to be sure, it is a
sophisticated guess, but a guess it is. This example makes the
point: the "system," meaning the computers in the kitchen,
doesn't know anything. It simply makes guesses—statistically
plausible guesses based on the designer's observations and
hunches. But these computer systems can't know what the person really has in mind.

To be fair, even statistical regularity can be useful. In this particular case, the kitchen doesn't take any action. Rather, it gets
ready to act, projecting a likely set of alternative actions on the
counter so that if by chance one of them is what you are planning to do, you only have to touch and indicate yes. If the system doesn't anticipate what you had in mind, you can just
ignore it—if you can ignore a house that constantly flashes suggestions to you on the counters, walls, and floors.

The system uses CommonSense (any confusion with the English term "common sense" is deliberate). Just as Common-
Sense is not really a word, the kitchen doesn't actually have any
real common sense. It only has as much sense as the designers
were able to program into it, which isn't much, given that it
can't really know what is going on.

But what if you decide to do something that the house thinks is bad for you, or perhaps simply wrong? "No," says the house, "that's not the proper way to cook that. If you do it that way, I can't be responsible for the result. Here, look at this cookbook. See? Don't make me say 'I told you so.'" This scenario has shades of *Minority Report*, the Steven Spielberg movie based upon the great futurist Philip K. Dick's short story by that name. As the hero, John Anderton, flees from the authorities, he passes through the crowded shopping malls. The advertising signs recognize him, calling him by name, tempting him with offers of clothes and special sale prices just for him. A car advertisement calls out, "It's not just a car, Mr. Anderton. It's an environment, designed to soothe and caress the tired soul." A travel agency entices him: "Stressed out, John Anderton? Need a vacation? Come to Aruba!" Hey, signs, he's running away from the cops; he isn't going to stop and buy some clothes.

Minority Report was fiction, but the technology depicted in the movie was designed by clever, imaginative experts who were very careful to depict only plausible technologies and activities. Those active advertising signs are already close to becoming a reality. Billboards in multiple cities recognize owners of BMW's Mini Cooper automobile by the RFID tags they carry. The Mini Cooper advertisements are harmless, and each driver has volunteered and selected the phrases that will be displayed. But now that this has started, where will it stop? Today, the billboard requires its audience to carry RFID tags, but this is a temporary expedient. Already, researchers are hard at work, using television cameras to view people and automobiles, then to identify them by their gait and facial features or their model, year, color, and license plate. This is how the City of London keeps track of cars that enter the downtown area. This is how security agencies expect to be able to track suspected terrorists. And this is how advertising agencies will track down potential customers. Will signs in shopping malls offer special bargains for frequent shoppers? Will restaurant menus offer your favorite meals? First in a science fiction story, then in a movie, then on the city streets: look for them at your nearest shops. Actually, you won't have to look: they will be looking for you.

Communicating with Our Machines: We Are Two Different Species

I can imagine it now: it's the middle of the night, but I can't sleep. I quietly get out of bed, careful not to wake up my wife, deciding that as long as I can't sleep, I might as well do some work. But my house detects my movement and cheerfully announces "good morning" as it turns on the lights and starts the radio news station. The noise wakes my wife: "Why are you waking me up so early?" she mumbles.

In this scenario, how could I explain to my house that behavior perfectly appropriate at one time is not so at another? Should I program it according to the time of day? No, sometimes my wife and I need to wake up early, perhaps to catch a morning flight. Or I might have a telephone conference with colleagues in India. For the house to know how to respond appropriately, it would need to understand the context, the reasoning behind the actions. Am I waking up deliberately? Does my wife still want to sleep? Do I really want the radio and the coffeemaker turned on? For the house to understand the reasons behind my awakening, it would have to know my intentions, but that requires effective communication at a level not possible today or in the near future. For now, automatic, intelligent devices must still be controlled by people. In the worst of cases, this can lead to conflict. In the best of cases, the human+machine forms a symbiotic unit, functioning well. Here, we could say that it is humans who make machines smart.

The technologists will try to reassure us that all technologies start off as weak and underpowered, that eventually their deficits are overcome and they become safe and trustworthy. At one level they are correct. Steam engines and steamships used to explode; they seldom do anymore. Early aircraft crashed frequently. Today, they hardly ever do. Remember Jim's problem with the cruise control that regained speed in an inappropriate location? I am certain that this particular situation can be avoided in future designs by coupling the speed control with the navigation system, or perhaps by developing systems in which the roads themselves transmit the allowable speeds to the cars (hence, no more ability to exceed speed limits), or better yet, by having the car itself determine safe speeds given the road, its curvature, slipperiness, and the presence of other traffic or people.

I am a technologist. I believe in making lives richer and more rewarding through the use of science and technology. But that is not where our present path is taking us. Today we are confronting a new breed of machines with intelligence and autonomy, machines that can indeed take over for us in many situations. In many cases, they will make our lives more effective, more fun, and safer. In others, however, they will frustrate us, get in our way, and even increase danger. For the first time, we have machines that are attempting to interact with us socially.

The problems that we face with technology are fundamental. They cannot be overcome by following old pathways. We need a calmer, more reliable, more humane approach. We need augmentation, not automation.

CHAPTER TWO

The Psychology of People & Machines

Three scenarios are possible now:

- "Pull up! Pull up!" cries the airplane to the pilots when it decides that the airplane is too low for safety.
- "Beep, beep," signals the automobile, trying to get the driver's attention, while tightening the seat belts, straightening the seat backs, and pretensing the brakes. It is watching the driver with its video camera, and because the driver is not paying attention to the road, it applies the brakes.
- "Bing, bing," goes the dishwasher, signaling that the dishes are clean, even if it is 3 a.m. and the message serves no purpose except to wake you up.

Three scenarios likely to be possible in the future:

- "No," says the refrigerator. "Not eggs again. Not until your weight comes down, and your cholesterol levels are lower. Scale tells me you still have to lose about five pounds, and the clinic keeps pinging me about your cholesterol. This is for your own good, you know."

• "I just checked your appointments diary in your smart phone," says the automobile as you get into the car after a day's work. "You have free time, so I've programmed that scenic route with those curves you like so much instead of the highway—I know you'll enjoy driving it. Oh, and I've picked your favorite music to go with it."

• "Hey," says your house one morning as you prepare to leave. "What's the rush? I took out the garbage. Won't you even say thank you? And can we talk about that nice new controller I've been showing you pictures of? It would make me much more efficient, and you know, the Jones's house already has one."

Some machines are obstinate. Others are temperamental. Some are delicate, some rugged. We commonly apply human attributes to our machines, and often these terms are fittingly descriptive, even though we use them as metaphors or similes. The new kinds of intelligent machines, however, are autonomous or semiautonomous: they create their own assessments, make their own decisions. They no longer need people to authorize their actions. As a result, these descriptions no longer are metaphors—they have become legitimate characterizations.

The first three scenarios I've depicted are already real. Airplane warning systems do indeed cry out, "Pull up!" (usually with a female voice). At least one automobile company has announced a system that monitors the driver with its video camera. If the driver does not appear to be watching the road when its forward-looking radar system senses a potential collision, it sounds an alarm—not with a voice (at least, not yet), but with buzzers and vibration. If the driver still does not respond, the system automatically applies the brakes and prepares the car for a crash. And I have already been awakened in the middle of the night by my dishwasher's beeps, anxious to tell me that the dishes have been cleaned.

Much is known about the design of automated systems. Slightly less is known about the interaction between people and these systems, although this too has been a topic of deep study for the past several decades. But these studies have dealt with industrial and military settings, where people were using the machines as part of their jobs. What about everyday people who might have no training, who might only use any particular machine occasionally? We know almost nothing of this situation, but this is what concerns me: untrained, everyday people, you and me, using our household appliances, our entertainment systems, and our automobiles.

How do everyday people learn how to use the new generation of intelligent devices? Hah! In bits and pieces, by trial and error, with endless feelings of frustration. The designers seem to believe that these devices are so intelligent, so perfect in their operation, that no learning is required. Just tell them what to do and get out of the way. Yes, the devices always come with instruction manuals, often big, thick, heavy ones, but these manuals are neither explanatory nor intelligible. Most do not even attempt to explain how the devices work. Instead, they give magical, mystical names to the mechanisms, oftentimes using nonsensical marketing terms, stringing the words together as in "SmartHomeSensor," as if naming something explains it.

The scientific community calls this approach "automagical": automatic plus magical. The manufacturer wants us to believe in—and trust—the magic. Even when things work well, it is somewhat discomforting to have no idea of how or why. The real problems begin when things go wrong, for then we have no idea how to respond. We are in the horrors of the in-between world. On the one hand, we are far from the science fiction, movieland world populated by autonomous, intelligent robots that always work perfectly. On the other hand, we are moving rapidly away from the world of manual control, one with no automation, where people operate equipment and get the task done.

"We are just making your life easier," the companies tell me, "healthier, safer, and more enjoyable. All those good things." Yes, if the intelligent, automatic devices worked perfectly, we would be happy. If they really were completely reliable, we wouldn't have to know how they work: automagic would then be just fine. If we had manual control over a task with manual devices that we understood, we would be happy. When, however, we get stuck in the in-between world of automatic devices we don't understand and that don't work as expected, not doing the task we wish to have done, well, then our lives are not made easier, and certainly not more enjoyable.

A Brief Introduction to the Psychology of People and Machines

The history of intelligent machines starts with early attempts to develop mechanical automatons, including clockworks and chess-playing machines. The most successful early chess-playing automaton was Wolfgang von Kempelen's "Turk," introduced with much fanfare and publicity to the royalty of Europe in 1769. In reality, it was a hoax, with an expert chess player cleverly concealed inside the mechanism, but the fact that the hoax succeeded so well indicates people's willingness to believe that mechanical devices could indeed be intelligent. The real growth in the development of smart machines didn't start until the mid 1900s with the development of control theory, servomechanisms and feedback, cybernetics, and information and automata theory. This occurred along with the rapid development of electronic circuits and computers, whose power has doubled roughly every two years. Because we've been doing this for more than forty years, today's circuits are one million times more powerful than those first, early "giant brains." Think of what will happen in twenty years, when machines are a thousand times more powerful than they are today—or in forty years, when they will be a million times more powerful.

The first attempts to develop a science of artificial intelligence (AI) also began in the mid 1900s. AI researchers moved the development of intelligent devices from the world of cold, hard, mathematical logic and decision making into the world of soft, ill-defined, human-centered reasoning that uses common-sense reasoning, fuzzy logic, probabilities, qualitative reasoning, and heuristics ("rules of thumb") rather than precise algorithms. As a result, today's AI systems can see and recognize objects, understand some spoken and written language, speak, move about the environment, and do complex reasoning.

Perhaps the most successful use of AI today for everyday activities is in computer games, developing intelligent characters who play against people, creating those intelligent, exasperating personalities in simulation games that seem to enjoy doing things to frustrate their creator, the game player. AI is also used successfully to catch bank and credit card fraud and other suspicious activities. Automobiles use AI for braking, stability control, lane keeping, automatic parking, and other features. In the home, simple AI controls the washing machines and driers, sensing the type of clothing and how dirty the load, adjusting things appropriately. In the microwave oven, AI can sense when food is cooked. Simple circuits in digital cameras and camcorders help control focus and exposure, including detecting faces, the better to track them even if they are moving and to adjust the exposure and focus to them appropriately. With time, the power and reliability of these AI circuits will increase, while their cost will decrease, so they will show up in a wide variety of devices, not just the most expensive ones. Remember, computer power has a thousandfold increase every twenty years, a million every forty.

Machine hardware is, of course, very different from that of animals. Machines are mostly made of parts with lots of straight lines, right angles, and arcs. There are motors and displays, control linkages and wires. Biology prefers flexibility: tissue, ligaments, and muscles. The brain works through massively parallel computational mechanisms, probably both chemical and electrical, and by settling into stable states. Machine brains, or, more accurately, machine information processing, operates much more quickly than biological neurons but also much less parallel in operation. Human brains are robust, reliable, and creative, marvelously adept at recognizing patterns. We humans tend to be creative, imaginative, and very adaptable to changing circumstances. We find similarities among events, and we use metaphorical expansion of concepts to develop whole new realms of knowledge. Furthermore, human memory, although imprecise, finds relationships and similarities among items that machines would not think of as similar at all. And, finally, human common sense is fast and powerful, whereas machine common sense does not exist.

The evolution of technology is very different from the natural evolution of animals. With mechanical systems, the evolution is entirely up to the designer who analyzes existing systems and makes modifications. Machines have evolved over the centuries, in part because our understanding and ability to invent and develop technology has continually improved, in part because the sciences of the artificial have developed, and in part because human needs, and the environment itself, have changed.

There is, however, one interesting parallel between the evolution of humans and that of intelligent, autonomous machines. Both must function effectively, reliably, and safely in the real world. The world itself, therefore, imposes the same demands and requirements upon all creatures: animal, human, and artificial. Animals and people have evolved complex systems of perception and action, emotion and cognition. Machines need analogous systems. They need to perceive the world and act upon it. They need to think and make decisions, to solve problems and reason. And yes, they need something akin to the emotional processes of people. No, not the same emotions that people have but the machine equivalents—the better to survive the hazards and dangers of the world, take advantage of opportunities, anticipate the consequences of their actions, and reflect upon what has happened and what is yet to come, thereby learning and improving performance. This is true for all autonomous, intelligent systems, animal, human, and machine.

The Rise of a New Organism—a Hybrid of Machine+Person

FIGURE 2.1

Car+driver: a new hybrid organism. *Rrrun*, a sculpture by Marta Thoma.

Photographed by the author from the Palo Alto, California, art collection at the Palo Alto Bowden Park.

For years, researchers have shown that a three-level description of the brain is useful for many purposes, even if it is a radical simplification of its evolution, biology, and operation. These three-level descriptions have all built upon the early, pioneering description of the "triune" brain by Paul McLean, where the three levels move up from lower structures of the brain (the brainstem) to higher ones (the cortex and frontal cortex), tracing both the evolutionary history and the power and sophistication of brain processing. In my book *Emotional Design*, I further simplified that analysis for use by designers and engineers. Think of the brain as having three levels of processing:

- *Visceral*: The most basic, the processing at this level is automatic and subconscious, determined by our biological heritage.
- *Behavioral*: This is the home of learned skills, but still mostly subconscious. This processing level initiates and controls much of our behavior. One important contribution is to manage expectations of the results of our actions.
- *Reflective*: This is the conscious, self-aware part of the brain, the home of the self and one's self-image, which does analyses of our past and prospective fantasies that we hope—or fear—might happen.

Were we to build these emotional states into machines, they would provide the same benefits to machines as their states provide us: rapid responses to avoid danger and accident, safety features for both the machines and any people who might be near, and powerful learning cues to improve expectations and enhance performance. Some of this is already happening. Elevators quickly jerk back their doors when they detect an obstacle (usually a recalcitrant human) in their path. Robotic vacuum cleaners avoid sharp drop-offs: fear of falling is built into their circuitry. These are visceral responses: the automatic fear responses prewired into humans through biology and prewired into machines by their designers. The reflective level of emotions places credit or blame upon our experiences. Machines are not yet up to this level of processing, but some day they will be, which will add even more power to their ability to learn and to predict.

The future of everyday things lies in products with knowledge, with intelligence, products that know where they are located and who their owners are and that can communicate with other products and the environment. The future of products is all about the capabilities of machines that are mobile, that can physically manipulate the environment, that are aware of both the other machines and the people around them and can communicate with them all.

By far the most exciting of our future technologies are those that enter into a symbiotic relationship with us: machine+person. Is the car+driver a symbiosis of human and machine in much the same way as the horse+rider might be? After all, the car+driver splits the processing levels, with the car taking over the visceral level and the driver the reflective level, both sharing the behavioral level in analogous fashion to the horse+rider.

Just as the horse is intelligent enough to take care of the visceral aspects of riding (avoiding dangerous terrain, adjusting its pace to the quality of the terrain, avoiding obstacles), so too is the modern automobile able to sense danger, controlling the car's stability, braking, and speed. Similarly, horses learn behaviorally complex routines for navigating difficult terrain or jumping obstacles, for changing canter when required and

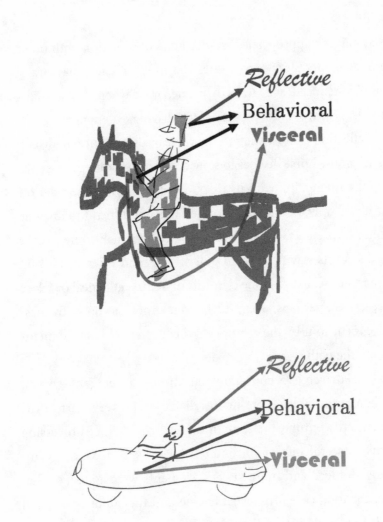

Figure 2.2

Horse+rider and car+driver as symbiotic systems. A horse+rider can be treated as a symbiotic system, with the horse providing visceral-level guidance and the driver the reflective level, with both overlapping at the behavioral level. So, too, can a car+driver be thought of as a symbiotic system, with the car increasingly taking over the visceral level, the driver the reflective level. And, once again, with a lot of overlap at the behavioral level. Note that in both cases, the horse or the intelligent car also tries to exert control at the reflective level.

maintaining appropriate distance and coordination with other horses or people. So, too, does the modern car behaviorally modify its speed, keep to its own lane, brake when it senses danger, and control other aspects of the driving experience.

Reflection is mostly left to the rider or driver, but not always, as when the horse decides to slow down or go home, or, not liking the interaction with its rider, decides to throw the rider off or just simply to ignore him or her. It is not difficult to imagine some future day when the car will decide which route to take and steer its way there or to pull off the road when it thinks it time to purchase gasoline or for its driver to eat a meal or take a break—or, perhaps, when it has been enticed to do so by messages sent to it by the roadway and commercial establishments along the path.

Car+driver is a conscious, emotional, intelligent system. When automobiles were first available at the very start of the twentieth century, the human driver provided all processing levels: visceral, behavioral, and reflective. As the technology improved, more and more visceral elements were added, so that the car took care of internal engine and fuel adjustments and shifting. With antiskid braking, stability controls, cruise control, and now lane-keeping functionality, the car has taken on more and more of the behavioral side of driving. So, with most modern cars, the car provides the visceral part, and the driver the reflective part, with both active at the behavioral level.

The twenty-first-century automobile has more and more reflective components: the conscious, reflective parts of the car+driver are being taken over by the car itself. The reflective powers are evident in the adaptive cruise control that continually assesses how close the car is to other vehicles, navigation systems that monitor how well the driver conforms to instructions, and all systems that monitor the driver's behavior. When the car's reflective analyses find problems, they signal the person to change behavior or just simply correct it when possible—but the car will take over complete control when it determines that this is required.

Someday cars will no longer need drivers. Instead, people will all be passengers, able to gossip, read, or even sleep while the car chauffeurs them to their destination. Do you enjoy driving? Fine, there will be special places set aside for people to drive their cars, just as those who enjoy horseback riding today have special places set aside for that activity. When this day arrives, and I expect it to happen some time in the twenty-first century, the entity known as car+driver will be extinct. Instead, we will have cars, and we will have people, just as we used to, except now the car will be visceral, behavioral, and reflective: a truly intelligent, autonomous machine, at least for the purposes of transportation, which will include not only the navigation and driving but also taking care of the comfort and well-being of the passengers, providing the right lighting, temperature, food and drink, and entertainment.

Will passengers be able to have meaningful conversations with their cars? In the past, the human tendency to assign beliefs, emotions, and personality traits to all sorts of things has been criticized as anthropomorphism. As machines gain in their cognitive and emotional capacities, the anthropomorphism may not be so erroneous. These assignments might very well be appropriate and correct.

The Gulfs of Goals, Action, and Perception

People have many unique capabilities that cannot be replicated in machines—at least not yet. As we introduce automation and intelligence into the machines we use today, we need to be humble and to recognize the problems and the potential for failure. We also need to recognize the vast discrepancy between the workings of people and of machines.

Today, there are "intelligent systems" in many everyday things. We have intelligent washing machines, dishwashers, robot vacuum cleaners, automobiles, computers, telephones, and computer games. Are these systems really intelligent? No, they are responsive. The intelligence is all in the heads of the design team, people who carefully try to anticipate all possible conditions and program into the system the appropriate responses. In other words, the design team is mind reading, trying to assess all of the possible future states and how a person would respond in each situation. On the whole, these responsive systems are valuable and helpful—but they often fail.

Why the failure? Because these systems can seldom measure directly the object of interest: they can only measure things their sensors can detect. Human beings have an incredibly rich sensorimotor system that allows continuous assessment of the state of the world and of our own bodies. We have tens of millions of specialized nerve cells for detecting light and sound, touch and taste, feel and balance, temperature and pressure, and pain, and internal sensors for our muscles and body position. In addition, we have built up complex representations of the world and our actions upon it, as well as accurate expectations based upon a long history of interaction. Machines don't even come close.

Machines' sensors are not only limited, but they measure different things from those of people. Psychological perception is not the same as physical sensing. Machines can detect light frequencies, infrared and radio waves that people cannot. They can detect sound frequencies that lie outside the range of human perception. The same is true for many other variables, as well as for action systems. We humans have flexible muscles and limbs, with dexterous fingers and toes. Machines are much less flexible but also more powerful.

Finally, people's goals are very different from those of machines. Indeed, many people would even deny that machines have goals. As machines get smarter and smarter, more and more intelligent, however, they will assess the situation and decide upon a course of action, with some distinct goals that they wish to accomplish. As for emotions, well, human emotions are central to our behavior and interpretation of the world. Machine emotions don't exist, and even when machines do start to have rudimentary emotions, they will differ considerably from those of people.

Common Ground: The Fundamental Limitation in Human-Machine Interaction

> Alan and Barbara begin with a great mass of knowledge, beliefs, and suppositions they believe they share. This is what I call their common ground. . . . [T]hey assume to be common ground what has taken place in conversations

> they have jointly participated in, including the current
> conversation so far. The more time Alan and Barbara
> spend together, the larger their common ground. . . .
> [T]hey cannot coordinate their actions without rooting
> them in their common ground.
>
> —Herbert Clark, *Using Language.*

Communication and negotiation require what linguists call a "common ground": a shared basis of understanding that serves as the platform for the interaction. In the quotation by the psycholinguist Herbert Clark, above, the fictitious couple, Alan and Barbara, involve their shared common ground in all joint activities, whether linguistic or not. When people from the same culture and social group interact, their shared beliefs and experiences allow for rapid and efficient interactions. Ever eavesdrop on the conversations of others? I do it often while walking through shopping malls and parks, in the name of science, of course. I am continually amazed by the lack of content, even between two people heavily engaged in discussion. A typical conversation might go like this:

Alan: "You know?"
Barbara: "Yeah."

To Alan and Barbara this interchange might very well be deep and significant. You and I will never know because all the critical knowledge we need to understand what is being referred to is missing: their common ground is unavailable to us.

The lack of common ground is the major cause of our inability to communicate with machines. People and machines have so little in common that they lack any notion of common ground. People and people? Machine and machine? That's different: those pairs function quite well. People can share with other people. Machines can share with other machines. But people and machines? Nope.

It might surprise you to hear that machines can share common ground with one another, but that is because their designers, usually engineers, spend a lot of time to ensure that all the background information required for efficient communication is indeed shared. When two machines start to interact, they first go through a ritual to ensure that there is mutual agreement about shared information, states, and even the syntax of the interaction. In the jargon of communication engineers, this is called "handshaking." This is so important that the engineering world has developed a huge framework of international committees to develop worldwide standards to ensure that communicating devices share the same assumptions and background knowledge. Standards are difficult to work out, for they require complex negotiations among otherwise competing companies, with technical, legal, political issues all having to be resolved. The end results are worth it, however: they establish the common language, protocols, and background knowledge required for the establishment of a common ground and, therefore, for effective communication.

Want an example of how two machines establish common ground? Although the handshaking is usually quiet and invisible to us humans, it is involved in almost every use of electronic devices that wish to communicate with another, whether it is your television set talking to the cable box and the cable box to the transmitting equipment, your computer connecting to a website, or your cell phone searching for a signal when you first turn it on. The most accessible example, however, comes from all those peculiar sounds that come out of a fax machine. After you have dialed the phone number (note that the dial tone and ringing sounds are also forms of handshaking), you then hear a series of warbling tones as your fax machine negotiates with the receiving machine what coding standard to use, what transmission rate, and what resolution on the page. Then, as the fax proceeds, one machine transmits the signals, and the other continually acknowledges correct receipt. It's a more restricted and mechanized version of the interaction between two people meeting for the first time as they try to figure out whom they know in common and what skills and interests they might share.

People can share common ground with other people. Machines can negotiate a common ground with other machines. But machines and people inhabit two different universes, one of logically proscribed rules that govern their interaction, the other of intricate, context-dependent actions, where the same apparent condition will give rise to different actions because "circumstances are different." Moreover, the fundamental gulfs of goals, actions, and perception mean that machines and people will not even be able to agree upon such fundamental things as, What is happening in the world? What actions can we take? What are we trying to accomplish? The lack of common ground is a supergulf, keeping machines and humans far apart.

People learn from their pasts, modifying their behavior to account for what they have learned. This also means that the common ground between people grows over time. Moreover, people are sensitive to which activities have been shared, so that Alan may interact with Barbara quite differently than he does with Charles, even in similar circumstances, because Alan realizes that the common ground he shares with Barbara is quite different from what he shares with Charles. Alan, Charles, and Barbara have the capacity to exchange new information; they can learn from their experiences and modify their behavior accordingly.

In contrast, machines can barely learn. Yes, they can make modifications in their performance as they experience success or failure, but their ability to generalize is very weak and, except in a few laboratory systems, pretty much nonexistent. Machine capabilities are continually improving, of course; throughout the world, research laboratories are working on all of these issues. But the gulf between what people have in common with one another and what machines and people have in common is huge and unlikely to be bridged in the foreseeable future.

Consider the three opening scenarios of future capabilities that started this chapter. Are they possible? How can machines know a person's private thoughts? How can they know what other activities are happening outside the range of their sensors? How can machines share enough knowledge about people to be so cocky in their suggestions? The answer is, they can't.

My refrigerator won't let me eat eggs? Maybe I'm not going to eat them; maybe I'm cooking for someone else. Yes, the refrigerator could detect that I was removing eggs, could know my weight and cholesterol levels through a medical information network that included both my home and some parts of my medical record from my physician's office, but that still doesn't give it the ability to read my mind and determine my intentions.

Can my automobile check my schedule and select an inter-esting route for me to drive? Yes, everything in that scenario is possible except, perhaps, the natural language interaction, but systems that speak are getting pretty good, so I wouldn't rule that out. Would I agree with the choice? If the car acted as de-scribed, it wouldn't matter: it is presenting an interesting sug-gestion, one I might not have thought of, but allowing me to choose. That's a nice, friendly interaction, one I certainly ap-prove of.

Could my house actually be jealous of other nearby homes? This is unlikely, although comparing the equipment and opera-tion of nearby homes is a perfectly sensible way to keep up to date. In businesses, this is called "benchmarking" and following "best practices." So, once again, the scenario is possible, al-though not necessarily with the same jaunty language.

Machines are very limited in learning and predicting the consequences of new interactions. Their designers have incor-porated whatever limited sensors their budget and the state of technology will allow. Beyond that, the designers are forced to imagine how the world might appear to the machine. From the limited data provided by the sensors, the designers must infer what might actually be going on and what actions the machine ought to take. Many of these systems do remarkably well as long as the task is well constrained and there are no unexpected oc-currences. Once the situation goes outside the simple parame-ters for which they were designed, their simple sensors and intelligent decision-making and problem-solving routines are simply insufficient for the task. The gulf that separates people from machines is immense.

The fundamental restriction on people's successful interactions with machines is the lack of common ground, but systems that avoid this danger, that suggest rather than demand, that allow people to understand and choose rather than confronting them with unintelligible actions, are perfectly sensible. The lack of common ground precludes many conversationlike interactions, but if the assumptions and commonalities are made clear, perhaps through implicit behavior and natural interactions that are readily interpreted by both machines and people, why then, I'm all for it. And this is the topic of chapter 3.

FIGURE 3.1

Kettle with whistle. A simple technology that summons us to do its bidding: Hear my whistle? Come and take care of me.

*Photograph © Daniel Hurst. Used under license
from Acclaim Images™.*

Natural Interaction

Whistles signal. People communicate. The difference is profound. Designers may think their designs communicate, but, in fact, they only signal, for the communication only goes in one direction. We need a way of coordinating our activities, cooperating with autonomous machines, so that we can perform tasks together smoothly, pleasurably.

Natural Interaction: Lessons to Be Learned

Almost all modern devices come with an assortment of lights and beeping signals that alert us to some approaching event or act as alarms, calling our attention to critical events. In isolation, each is useful and helpful. But most of us have multiple devices, each with multiple signaling systems. The modern home and automobile can easily have dozens or even hundreds of potential signals. In industry and health care, the number of alerts and alarms increases dramatically. If the trend continues, the home of the future will be one continual wail of alerts and alarms. So, although each single signal may be informative and useful, the cacophony of the many is distracting, irritating, and, as a result, potentially dangerous. Even in the home, where danger is less often encountered, when many signals might be active, even the beep of one is unintelligible:

"Did I hear the washing machine beep?" asks my wife.

"I thought it was the dishwasher," I respond, scurrying from kitchen to laundry room and back again, trying to figure out which it was.

"Oh, it's the timer on the microwave oven. I forgot that I had set it to remind me when I had to make that phone call."

The devices of the future promise to move us into even more confusion and annoyance if they follow the same method of signaling used today. Yet, there is a better way, a system of natural interaction that can be more effective and simultaneously less annoying. We manage well in the natural world, interpreting the signs and signals of the environment and its inhabitants. Our perceptual system conveys a rich sense of space, created from the seamless combination of sights and sounds, smells and feelings that surround us. Our proprioceptive system conveys information from the semicircular canals of the inner ear and our muscles, tendons, and joints to give us a sense of body location and orientation. We identify events and objects rapidly, often from just minimal cues—a brief glimpse or sound, for instance. But more importantly for my purposes, natural signals inform without annoyance, providing a natural, nonintrusive, nonirritating, continuous awareness of the events around us.

Consider natural sounds, for example: not the beeps and buzzes of our equipment, not even speech sounds, but natural environmental sounds. Sounds convey a rich picture of the happenings around us because sounds are an automatic result whenever objects move, whenever they meet one another, scraping, colliding, pushing, or resisting. Sounds tell us where things are located in space, but they can also reveal their composition (leaves, branches, metal, wood, glass) and activity (falling, sliding, breaking, closing) as well. Even stationary objects contribute to our aural experience, for the way that sounds are reflected and shaped by environmental structures gives us a sense of space and our location within it. This is all done so automatically, so naturally, that we are often unaware of how much we depend upon sound for our spatial sense and for our knowledge of the events in the world.

There are lessons to be learned from these natural interactions with the real world. Although simple tones and flashes of white or colored light are the easiest ways for designers to add signals to our devices, they are also the least natural, least informative, and most irritating of means. A better way to design the future things of everyday life is to use richer, more informative, less intrusive signals: natural signals. Use rich, complex, natural lights and sounds so that people can tell whether a sound is in front or behind, up or down, what the material and composition is of visible objects, whether an expected event is near in time or far, critical or not. Not only are natural signals less intrusive, but they can be a lot more informative, always in the background making us, if only subconsciously, aware of the state of ongoing processes. They are easier to identify, so we no longer have to scurry about trying to find the source of the signal. Natural, yet providing continual awareness. The natural world of sound, color, and interaction is also the most satisfying. Want an example? Consider the whistling kettle.

The Sound of Boiling Water: Natural, Powerful, and Useful

The sound of water boiling in a kettle provides a good example of a natural, informative signal. This sound is produced by pockets of heated water moving about, creating sounds that change naturally until, at last, a rapid, "rolling" boil is reached, at which time the teakettle settles down to a continuous, pleasant sound. These activities allow a person to tell roughly how close the water is to boiling. Now, add a whistle to signal when boiling has taken place, not through some artificial electronic tone but by enclosing the airspace in the spout, letting a small amount escape through the opening. The result is a naturally produced whistle, one that starts slowly, at first weak and unsteady, then progresses to a loud, continuous sound. Does it take some learning to predict how much time is available at each stage of the process? Sure, but the learning is done without effort. After listening to the sounds of boiling water a few times, you get it. No fancy, expensive electronics. Simple, natural sound. Let this be a model for the other systems: always try to find some naturally occurring component of the system that can serve as an informative cue about the state of things. Maybe it is a vibration, maybe sound, maybe the way light changes.

In the automobile, it is possible to isolate the passenger compartment from most of the vibration and sounds. Although this might be a good idea for the passengers, it is a bad idea for the driver. Designers have had to work hard to reintroduce the outside environment in the form of "road feel" to the driver through sound and vibration of the steering wheel. If you use an electric drill, you know how important the sound of the motor and the feel of the drill are to accurate, precise drilling. Many cooks prefer gas ranges because they can more rapidly judge the degree of heat by the appearance of the flame than by the more abstract dials and indicators of the newer types of cooktops.

So far, all my examples of natural signals come from existing appliances and devices, but what about the world of future things, where autonomous intelligence increasingly takes control? Actually, if anything, these completely automatic devices provide even richer opportunities. The sounds of the little cleaning robot scurrying about the floor remind us that it is busy and let us subtly monitor its progress. Just as the pitch of the vacuum cleaner's motor naturally rises when items get stuck in its hose, the pitch of the robot's motors tells us how easy or hard it is finding the task. The problems with automation occur when something breaks down, turning the task over to people, often without warning. Well, with naturalistic, continual feedback, there will be warning.

Implicit Signals and Communication

Whenever I walk into a research laboratory, I look to see how neat or messy it is. When everything is orderly, everything in its place, I suspect this is a laboratory where not much work is being done. I like to see disorder: that means active, engaged people. Disorder is a natural, implicit sign of activity.

We leave traces of our activities: footprints in the sand, litter in the trash, books on desks, counters, and even the floor. In the academic field of semiotics, these are called signs or signals. To the reader of detective novels, they are called clues, and ever since the perceptive eye of Sherlock Holmes entered the world of detectives, they have provided the evidence of people's activities. These nonpurposeful clues are what the Italian cognitive scientist Cristiano Castlefranchi calls "implicit communication." Castlefranchi defines behaviorally implicit communication as natural side effects that can be interpreted by others. It "does not require a specific learning or training, or transmission," says Castlefranchi. "It simply exploits perceptual patterns of usual behavior and their recognition." Implicit communication is an important component of the design of intelligent things because it informs without interruption, annoyance, or even the need for conscious attention.

Footprints, disorderly research laboratories, underlining and sticky notes on reading matter, the sounds of elevators or of a home's appliances: all are natural, implicit signals that allow us to infer what is happening, to remain aware of the activities in the environment, to know when it is time to step in and take action and when it is possible to ignore them and continue with whatever we are doing.

A good example comes from the world of the old-fashioned telephone. In the old days, when making an international phone call, clicks and hisses and noises let you know that progress was being made, and through the differing sounds, you could even learn how well things were progressing. As equipment and technology got better, the circuits became quieter, until they became noise free. Oops, all the implicit clues were gone. People waiting on the line heard silence, which they sometimes interpreted to mean the call had failed, so they hung up. It was necessary to reintroduce sounds into the circuit so people would know that the call was still being processed. "Comfort noise" is what the engineers called it, their condescending way of responding to the needs of their customers. The sounds are far more than "comfort." They are implicit communication, confirming that the circuit is still active, informing the telephone caller that the system is still in the process of making the connection. And, yes, that implicit confirmation is reassuring, comforting.

Although sound is important for providing informative feedback, there is a downside. Sounds are often annoying. We have eyelids that permit us to shut out scenes we do not wish to watch: there are no earlids. Psychologists have even devised scales of annoyance for rating noise and other sounds. Unwanted sound can disrupt conversations, make it difficult to concentrate, and disturb tranquil moments. As a result, much effort has gone into the development of quieter devices in the office, factory, and home. The automobile has become so quiet that many years ago Rolls-Royce used to brag that "at 60 mph the loudest noise in this new Rolls-Royce comes from the electric clock."

Although quiet can be good, it can also be dangerous. Without noise from the environment, the automobile driver can't be aware of the sirens of emergency vehicles, or the honking of horns, or even the weather. If all roads feel equally smooth, regardless of their actual condition, regardless of how fast the car is traveling, how can the driver know what speed is safe? Sounds and vibrations provide natural indicators, implicit signals of important conditions. In electrically driven vehicles, the engine can be so silent that even the driver might be unaware that it is operating. Pedestrians subconsciously rely upon the implicit sounds of automobiles to keep them informed of nearby vehicles; as a result, they have on occasion been taken unawares by the silent, electrically propelled ones (or by any quiet vehicle, a bicycle, for example). It has become necessary to add a signal inside the automobile to remind the driver that the engine is running (alas, one manufacturer does this most unnaturally by using a beeping sound). It is even more important to add some naturalistic sounds outside the vehicle. The Federation for the Blind, an organization whose members have already been affected by the silence of these vehicles, has suggested adding something in the car's wheel well or on the axle that would make a sound when the car was moving. If done properly, this could produce a natural-sounding cue that would vary with the speed of the vehicle, a desirable attribute.

Because sound can be both informative and annoying, this raises the difficult design problem of understanding how to enhance its value while minimizing its annoyance. In some cases, this can be done by trying to minimize distasteful sounds, lowering their intensity, minimizing the use of rapid transients, and trying to create a pleasant ambience. Subtle variations in this background ambience might yield effective communication.

One designer, Richard Sapper, created a kettle whose whistle produced a pleasant musical chord: the musical notes E and B. Note that even annoyance has its virtues: emergency signals, such as those of ambulances, fire trucks, and alarms for fire, smoke, or other potential disasters, are deliberately loud and annoying, the better to attract attention.

Sound should still be used where it appears to be a natural outgrowth of the interaction, but arbitrary, meaningless sounds are almost always annoying. Because sound, even when cleverly used, can be so irritating, in many cases its use should be avoided. Sound is not the only alternative: sight and touch provide alternative modalities.

Mechanical knobs can contain tactile cues, a kind of implicit communication, for their preferred settings. For example, in some rotating tone controls you can feel a little "blip" as you rotate it past the preferred, neutral position. The controls in some showers will not go above a preset temperature unless the user manipulates a button that enables higher temperatures. The "blip" in the tone control allows someone to set it to the neutral position rapidly and efficiently. The stop in the shower serves as a warning that higher temperatures might be uncomfortable, or even dangerous, for some people. Some commercial airplanes use a similar stop on their throttles: when the throttles are pushed forward, they stop at the point where higher throttle setting might damage the engines. In an emergency, however, if the pilot believes it is necessary to go beyond in order to avoid a crash, the pilot can force the throttle beyond the first stopping point. In such a case, damage to the engine is clearly of secondary importance.

Physical marks provide another possible direction. When we read paper books and magazines, we may leave marks of our progress, whether through normal wear and tear or by deliberate folding of pages, insertion of sticky notes, highlighting, underlining, and margin notes. In electronic documents, all of these cues don't have to be lost. After all, the computer knows what has been read, what pages have been scrolled to, which sections have been read. Why not make wear marks on the software, letting the reader discover which sections have been edited, commented upon, or read the most? The research team of Will Hill, Jim Hollan, Dave Wroblewski, and Tim McCandless have done just that, adding marks on electronic documents so that viewers can find which sections have been looked at the most. Dirt and wear have their virtues as natural indicators of use, relevance, and importance. Electronic documents can borrow these virtues without the deficits of dirt, squalor, and damage to the material. Implicit interaction is an interesting way to develop intelligent systems. No language, no forcing: simple clues in both directions indicate recommended courses of action.

Implicit communication can be a powerful tool for informing without annoying. Another important direction is to exploit the power of affordances, the subject of the next section.

Affordances as Communication

It started off with an e-mail: Clarisse de Souza, a professor of informatics in Rio de Janeiro wrote to disagree with my definition of "affordance." "Affordance," she told me, "is really communication between the designer and the user of a product." "No," I wrote back. "An affordance is simply a relationship that exists in the world: it is simply there. Nothing to do with communication."

I was wrong. She was not only right, but she got me to spend a delightful week in Brazil, convincing me, then went on to expand upon her idea in an important book, *Semiotic Engineering*. I ended up a believer: "Once designs are thought of as shared communication and technologies as media, the entire design philosophy changes radically, but in a positive and constructive way," is what I wrote about the book for its back cover.

To understand this discussion, let me back up a bit and explain the original concept of an affordance and how it became part of the vocabulary of design. Let me start with a simple question: how do we function in the world? As I was writing *The Design of Everyday Things*, I pondered this question: when we encounter something new, most of the time we use it just fine, not even noticing that it is a unique experience. How do we do this? We encounter tens of thousands of different objects throughout our lives, yet in most cases, we know just what to do with them, without instruction, without any hesitation. When faced with a need, we are often capable of designing quite novel solutions; "hacks" they are sometimes called: folded paper under a table leg to stabilize the table, newspapers pasted over a window to block the sun. Years ago, as I pondered this question, I realized that the answer had to do with a form of implicit communication, a form of communication that today we call "affordances."

The term *affordance* was invented by the great perceptual psychologist J. J. Gibson to explain our perceptions of the world. Gibson defined affordances as the range of activities that an animal or person can perform upon an object in the world. Thus, a chair affords sitting, supporting, throwing, and hiding behind for an adult human, but not for a young child, an ant, or an elephant. Affordances are not fixed properties: they are relationships that hold between objects and agents. Moreover, to Gibson, affordances existed whether they were obvious or not, visible or not, or even whether or not anyone had ever discovered it. Whether or not you knew about it was irrelevant.

I took Gibson's term and showed how it can be applied to the practical problems of design. Although Gibson didn't think they needed to be visible, to me, the critical thing was their visibility. If you didn't know that an affordance existed, I argued, then it was worthless, at least in the moment. In other words, the ability of a person to discover and make use of affordances is one of the important ways that people function so well, even in novel situations when encountering novel objects.

Providing effective, perceivable affordances is important in the design of today's things, whether they be coffee cups, toasters, or websites, but these attributes are even more important for the design of future things. When devices are automatic, autonomous, and intelligent, we need perceivable affordances to show us how we might interact with them and, equally importantly, how they might interact with the world. We need affordances that communicate: hence the importance of de Souza's discussion with me and of her semiotic approach to affordances.

The floor slopes gently, almost imperceptibly downward, drawing you toward the altar. . . . What makes this potent architecture is its ability to draw you through these spaces without any coercion. There is no single path, but you in-

tuitively know where to go. (*New York Times* review of St.
Pierre church in Firminy, France.)

Notice the phrase "you intuitively know where to go" from
the quotation: that is the power of visual, perceivable affordances. They guide behavior, and in the best of cases, they do so
without the person's awareness of the guidance—it just feels
natural. This is how we can interact so well with most of the objects around us. They are passive and responsive: they sit there
quietly, awaiting our activity. In the case of the church, we walk
down the aisle. In the case of appliances, such as a television set,
we push a button, and the television set changes channels. We
walk, turn, push, press, lift, and pull, and something happens. In
all these cases, the design challenge is to let us know beforehand
what range of operations is possible, what operation we need to
perform, and how we go about doing it. During the carrying
out of the action, we want to know how it is progressing. After-
ward, we want to know what change took place.

This description pretty much describes all the designed objects with which we interact today, from household appliances
to office tools, from computers to older automobiles, from websites and computer applications to complex mechanical devices.
The design challenges are large and not always carried out successfully, hence our frustrations with so many everyday objects.

Communicating with Autonomous, Intelligent Devices

The objects of the future will pose problems that cannot be
solved simply by making the affordances visible. Autonomous,

intelligent machines pose particular challenges, in part because the communication has to go both ways, from person to machine and from machine to person. How do we communicate back and forth with these machines? To answer this question, let's look at the wide range of machine+person coupling—an automobile, bicycle, or even a horse—and examine how that machine+person entity communicates with another machine+person entity.

In chapter 1, I described my discovery that my description of the symbiotic coupling of horse and rider was a topic of active research by scientists at the National Aeronautics and Space Administration's (NASA) Langley Research Center in Virginia and the Institut für Verkehrsführung und Fahr in Braunschweig, Germany. Their goal, like mine, is to enhance human-machine interaction.

When I visited Braunschweig to learn about their research, I also learned more about how to ride a horse. A critically important aspect of both horseback riding and of a driver's controlling a horse and carriage, Frank Flemisch, the director of the German group explained to me, is the distinction between "loose-rein" and "tight-rein" control. Under tight reins, the rider controls the horse directly, with the tightness communicating this intention to the horse. In loose-rein riding, the horse has more autonomy, allowing the rider to perform other activities or even to sleep. Loose and tight are the extremes on a continuum of control, with various intermediate stages. Moreover, even in tight-rein control, where the rider is in control, the horse can balk or otherwise resist the commands. Similarly, in loose-rein control, the person can still provide some oversight

FIGURE 3.2

Loose-rein guidance of a
horse and carriage. With
an intelligent horse providing
the power and guidance,
the driver can relax and not
even pay much attention to
the driving. This is loose-rein
control, where the horse has
taken over.

Photograph by the author
in Brugge, Belgium.

using the reins, verbal commands, pressure from the thighs and legs, and heel kicks.

An even closer analog of the interaction between horse and driver is that of a wagon or carriage, as in Figure 3.2. Here, the driver is not as tightly coupled to the horse as the rider who sits on its back, so this is more similar to the average, nonprofessional driver and a modern automobile. The coupling between horse and driver on the wagon, or driver and automobile, is restricted. Even here, though, the continuum between "tight-rein" and "loose-rein" control still applies. Note how the degree of animal autonomy or of human control is communicated by exploiting the implicit communication made possible through the affordances of the reins. Combining implicit communication with affordances is a powerful, very natural concept. This aspect of working with a horse is the critical component that can be borrowed in the design of machine+human systems—in designing the system so that the amount of independence and interaction can vary in a natural manner, capitalizing upon the affordances of the controller and the communicative capabilities it provides.

When I drove the automobile simulator at Braunschweig, the difference between "loose-" and "tight-rein" control was apparent. Under tight-rein conditions, I did most of the work, determining the force on the accelerator, brake, and steering wheel, but the car nudged me, this way or that, trying to keep me on a steady course within the highway's lane boundaries. If I got too close to the car ahead of me, the steering wheel pushed back, indicating that I should back off. Similarly, if I lagged behind too much, the steering wheel moved forward, urging me to speed up a bit. Under loose-rein conditions, the car was more aggressive in its actions, so much so that I hardly had to do anything at all. I had the impression that I could close my eyes and simply let the car guide me through the driving. Unfortunately, during the limited time available for my visit, I wasn't able to try everything I now realize I should have. The one thing missing from the demonstration was a way for the driver to select how much control to give to the system. This transition in amount of control is important, for when an emergency arises, it may be necessary to transfer the control very rapidly, without distracting from the attention required to deal with the situation.

The horse+rider conceptualization provides a powerful metaphor for the development of machine+human interfaces, but the metaphor alone is not enough. We need to learn more about these interfaces, and it is reassuring to see that research has already begun, with scientists studying how a person's intentions might best be communicated to the system, and vice versa.

One way for the system to communicate its goals and intentions to a person is through an explicit presentation of the strategy that is being followed. One research group, Christopher Miller and his colleagues, proposes that systems share a "playbook" with everyone involved. The group describes their work as "based on a shared model of the tasks in the domain. This model provides a means of human-automation communication about plans, goals, methods and resource usage—a process akin to referencing plays in a sports team's playbook. The Playbook enables human operators to interact with subordinate systems with the same flexibility as with well-trained human subordinates, thus allowing for adaptive automation." The idea is that the person can convey intentions by selecting a particular playbook for the automatic systems to follow, or if the automation is in control, it shows the playbook it has selected. These researchers are concerned with the control of airplanes, so the playbook might specify how it will control take off and the achievement of cruising altitude. Whenever the machine is working autonomously, controlling what is happening, it always displays the play that it is following, letting the human understand how the immediate actions fit into the overall scheme and change the choice of plays if necessary. A critical component here is the form by which the play is shown. A written description or a list of planned actions is not likely to be acceptable, requiring too much effort to process. For the playbook approach to be effective, especially for everyday people who do not wish to undergo training to accommodate the intelligent objects in their homes, a simple means of displaying the plays is essential.

I've seen similar concepts at work on the displays of large commercial copiers, where the display clearly shows the "playbook" being followed: perhaps 50 copies, duplex, two-sided copying, stapled, and sorted. I have seen nice graphical depictions, with the image of a piece of paper turning over, showing printing on both sides and how the printed page is combined with other pages so that it is easy to tell if it has been aligned properly, with the page flipped along the short edge or the long one, and with a depiction of the final stapled documents stacked up neatly in a pile, with the height of the pile showing how far the job has progressed.

When automation is operating relatively autonomously under loose-rein conditions, display schemes similar to the playbook are especially relevant to allow people to determine just what strategy the machine is following and how far along it is in its actions.

The Bicycles of Delft

Delft is a charming small town near the Atlantic coast of the Netherlands, home of the Technische Universiteit Delft, or in English, the Delft University of Technology. The streets are narrow, with several major canals encircling the business district. The walk from the hotel section to the university is picturesque, meandering past and over canals, through the narrow winding streets. The danger comes not from automobiles but from the swarms of bicycles, weaving their way at great speeds in all directions and, to my eyes, appearing out of nowhere. In Holland, bicycles have their own roadways, separate from the roads and pedestrian paths. But not in the central square of Delft. There, bicyclists and pedestrians mix.

FIGURE 3.3

Holland is the land of multiple bicycles, which, although environmentally friendly, present a traffic hazard to people trying to walk across the square. The rule is: Be predictable. Don't try to help the bicyclists. If you stop or swerve, they will run into you.

(Photograph by the author.)

"It's perfectly safe," my hosts kept reassuring me, "as long as you don't try to help out. Don't try to avoid the bikes. Don't stop or swerve. Be predictable." In other words, maintain a steady pace and a steady direction. The bicyclists have carefully calculated their course so as to miss one another and all the pedestrians under the assumption of predictability. If pedestrians try to outmaneuver the bicyclists, the results will be disastrous.

The bicyclists of Delft provide a model for how we might interact with intelligent machines. After all, here we have a person, the walker, interacting with an intelligent machine, a bicycle. In this case, the machine is actually the couplet of bicycle+person, with the person providing both the motive power and the intelligence. Both the person walking and the bicycle+person have the full power of the human mind controlling them; yet, these two cannot coordinate successfully. The combination bicycle+person doesn't lack intelligence: it lacks communication. There are many bicycles, each traveling quite a bit faster than the pace of the walker. It isn't possible to talk to the bicyclists because, by the time they are close enough for conversation, it is too late to negotiate. In the absence of effective communication, the way to interact is for the person walking to be predictable so that no coordination is required: only one of the participants, the bicycle+person has to do planning; only one has to act.

This story provides a good lesson for design. If a person cannot coordinate activities with an intelligent, human-driven machine, the bicycle+person, why would we ever think the situation would be any easier when the coordination must take place with an intelligent machine? The moral of this story is that we shouldn't even try. Smart machines of the future should not try to read the minds of the people with whom they interact, either to infer their motives or to predict their next actions. The problem with doing this is twofold: first, they probably will be wrong; second, doing this makes the machine's actions unpredictable. The person is trying to predict what the machine is going to do while, at the same time, the machine is trying to guess the actions of the person—a sure guarantee of confusion. Remember the bicycles of Delft. They illustrate an important rule for design: be predictable.

Now comes the next dilemma: which should be the predictable element, the person or the intelligent device? If the two elements were of equal capability and equal intelligence, it wouldn't matter. This is the case with the bicyclists and pedestrians. The intelligence of both comes from human beings, so it really doesn't matter whether it is the bicyclists who are careful to act predictably or the pedestrians. As long as everyone agrees who takes which role, things will probably work out okay. In most situations, however, the two components are not equal. The intelligence and general world knowledge of people far exceeds the intelligence and world knowledge of machines. People and bicyclists share a certain amount of common knowledge or common ground: their only difficulty is that there is not sufficient time for adequate communication and coordination. With a person and a machine, the requisite common ground does not exist, so it is far better for the machine to behave predictably and let the person respond appropriately. Here is where the playbook idea could be effective by helping people understand just what rules the machine is following.

Machines that try to infer the motives of people, that try to second-guess their actions, are apt to be unsettling at best, and in the worst case, dangerous.

Natural Safety

The second example illustrates how accident rate can be reduced by changing people's perception of safety. Call this "natural" safety, for it relies upon the behavior of people, not safety warnings, signals, or equipment.

Which airport has fewer accidents: an "easy" one that is flat, with good visibility and weather conditions (e.g., Tucson, in the Arizona desert) or a "dangerous" one with hills, winds, and a difficult approach (e.g., San Diego, California, or Hong Kong)?

Answer—the dangerous ones. Why? Because the pilots are alert, focused, and careful. One of the pilots of an airplane that had a near crash while attempting to land at Tucson told NASA's voluntary accident reporting system that "the clear, smooth conditions had made them complacent." (Fortunately, the terrain avoidance system alerted the pilots in time to prevent an accident. Remember the first example that opened chapter 2, where the plane said, "Pull up, Pull up," to the pilots? That's what saved them.) The same principle about perceived versus real safety holds with automobile traffic safety. The subtitle of a magazine article about the Dutch traffic engineer Hans Monderman makes the point: "Making driving seem more dangerous could make it safer."

People's behavior is dramatically impacted by their perception of the risk they are undergoing. Many people are afraid of flying but not of driving in an automobile or, for that matter, being struck by lightning. Well, driving in a car, whether as driver or passenger, is far riskier than flying as a passenger in a commercial airline. As for lightning, well, in 2006 there were three deaths in U.S. commercial aviation but around fifty deaths by lightning. Flying is safer than being out in a thunderstorm. Psychologists who study perceived risk have discovered that when an activity is made safer, quite often the accident rate does not change. This peculiar result has led to the hypothesis of "risk compensation": when an activity is changed so that it is perceived to be safer, people take more risks, thereby keeping the accident rate constant.

Thus, adding seat belts to cars, or helmets to motorcyclists, or protective padding to football uniforms, or higher, better fitting boots for skiers, or antiskid brakes and stability controls to automobiles leads people to change their behavior to keep risk the same. The same principle even applies to insurance: If they have insurance against theft, people aren't as careful with their belongings. Forest rangers and mountaineers have discovered that providing trained rescue squads has the tendency to increase the number of people who risk their lives because they now believe that if they get into trouble, they will be rescued.

Risk homeostasis is the term given to this phenomenon in the literature on safety. *Homeostasis* is the scientific term for systems that tend to maintain a state of equilibrium, in this case, a constant sense of safety. Make the environment appear safer, goes this hypothesis, and drivers will engage in riskier behavior, keeping the actual level of safety constant. This topic has been controversial since it was first introduced in the 1980s by the Dutch psychologist Gerald Wilde. The controversy surrounds the reasons for the effect and its size, but there is no doubt that the phenomenon itself is real. So, why not put this phenomenon to use in reverse? Why not make things safer by making them look more dangerous than they actually are?

Suppose that we got rid of traffic safety features: no more traffic lights, stop signs, pedestrian crossings, wider streets, or special bike paths. Instead, we might add roundabouts (traffic circles) and make streets narrower. The idea seems completely crazy; it reverses common sense. Yet, it is precisely what the Dutch traffic engineer Hans Monderman advocates for cities. Proponents of this method use the name "Shared Space" to describe their work with several successful applications across Europe: Ejby in Denmark, Ipswich in England, Ostende in Belgium, Makkinga and Drachten in the Netherlands. This philosophy does not change the need for signals and regulations on high-speed highways, but in small towns and even in restricted districts within large cities, the concept is appropriate. The group reports that in London, England, "Shared Space principles were used for the redesigning of the busy shopping street Kensington High Street. Because of the positive results (a 40% reduction in road accidents) the city council are going to apply Shared Space in Exhibition Road, the central artery in London's most important museum district." Here is how they describe their philosophy:

> Shared Space. That is the name of a new approach to pub-lic space design that is receiving ever-wider attention. The striking feature is the absence of conventional traffic man-agement measures, such as signs, road marking, humps and barriers, and the mixing of all traffic flows. "Shared Space gives people their own responsibility for what 'their' public space will look like and how they are going to be-have in it," says Mr. Hans Monderman, head of the Shared Space Expert Team.
>
> "The traffic is no longer regulated by traffic signs, people do the regulating themselves. And precisely that is the whole idea. Road users should take each other into ac-count and return to their everyday good manners. Experi-ence shows that the additional advantage is that the number of road accidents decreases in the process."

This concept of reverse risk compensation is a difficult policy to follow, and it takes a courageous city administration. Even though it might reduce accidents and fatalities overall, it can't prevent all accidents, and as soon as there is one fatality, anxious residents will argue for warning signs, traffic lights, special pedestrian paths, and widening of the streets. It is very difficult to sustain the argument that if it looks dangerous, it may actually be safer.

Why does making something look more dangerous actually make it safer? Several people have taken up the challenge of explaining this result. In particular, the British researchers Elliott, McColl, and Kennedy propose that the following cognitive mechanisms are involved:

- More complex environments tend to be associated with slower driving speeds, the likely mechanisms being increases in cognitive load and perceived risk.

- Natural traffic calming, such as a humpback bridge or a winding road, can be very effective in reducing speeds, as well as being more acceptable to drivers. Carefully designed schemes, using the properties of natural traffic calming, have the potential to achieve a similar effect.

- Emphasizing changes of environment (e.g., highway or village boundaries) can increase awareness, reduce speed, or both.

- Enclosing a distant view or breaking up linearity can reduce speeds.

- Creating uncertainty can reduce speeds.

- Combining measures tends to be more effective than implementing individual ones but can be visually intrusive and may be costly.

- Roadside activity (e.g., parked vehicles, pedestrians, or a cycle lane) can reduce speeds.

The leading causes of accidental injuries and death in the home include falls and poisoning. Why not apply the same counterintuitive concept of reverse risk compensation? What if we made dangerous activities look more dangerous? Suppose we simultaneously made bathtubs and showers look more slippery (while actually making them less so). Suppose we designed stairways to look more dangerous than they really are. We might make some ingestible items look more forbidding, especially poisons. Would amplifying the appearance of danger reduce the occurrence of accidents? Probably.

How might the principles of reverse risk compensation apply to the automobile? Today, the driver is bathed in comfort, acoustically isolated from road noise, physically isolated from vibration, warm, comfortable, listening to music, and interacting with passengers, or perhaps talking on the telephone. (In fact, studies show that talking on a mobile phone while driving, even a hands-free telephone, is just as dangerous as driving while drunk.) There is a distancing from the events, a loss of situation awareness. And with the development of automatic devices that take over stability, braking, and lane keeping, there is an even greater distance from reality.

Suppose, however, that the driver could be removed from that comfortable position and placed outside, much like the stage coach driver of an earlier era, exposed to the weather, to the rushing air, to the sights, sounds, and vibrations of the road. Obviously, drivers would not permit us to do this to them, but how can we get back situation awareness without necessarily subjecting the driver to the harsh outside environment? Today, through the car's computers, motors, and advanced mechanical systems, we can control not only how a car behaves but also how it feels to the driver. As a result, we could do a better job of coupling the driver to the situation in a natural manner, without requiring signals that need to be interpreted, deciphered, and acted upon.

Just imagine how you would feel if, while driving your car, the steering wheel suddenly felt loose, so that it became more difficult to control the car. Wouldn't you quickly become more alert, more concerned with maintaining a safe passage? What if we deliberately introduced this feeling? Wouldn't drivers become more cautious? This behavior is certainly possible in the design of some future car. More and more, automobiles are transitioning toward what is called "drive by wire," where the controls are no longer mechanically connected to anything other than a computer. This is how modern airplanes are controlled, and in many vehicles, the throttle and brakes already work in this way, passing signals to the automobile's many microprocessors. Someday, steering will be "by wire," with electric motors or hydraulic mechanisms providing feedback to the driver so that it will feel as if the driver is turning the wheels and feeling the road through the wheel's vibrations. When we reach this point, then it will be possible to mimic the feel of skidding, or heavy vibration, or even a loose, wobbly steering wheel. The neat thing about smart technology is that we could provide precise, accurate control, even while giving the driver the perception of loose, wobbly controllability.

The problem is that a wobbly steering wheel would make the driver think there was something the matter with the car. Not only would this send the wrong message, but it would never be acceptable to the automobile manufacturers. When I mentioned this to an engineering group at one major automobile company, the response was nervous laughter. "Why would we want to produce a product that sometimes felt as if it were failing to work properly?" they asked. Good point. Instead of making the car appear to be dangerous, however, we could make it appear that the environment was dangerous.

Picture someone driving over an old dirt highway, with deep ruts that capture the car, moving it in unpredictable ways: in such a situation, we wouldn't blame the car; we would blame the ruts in the road. Or consider driving through thick, heavy mud, which makes the automobile behave sluggishly and unable to respond with agility. Or, if driving on ice so that the car continually skidded, we would slow down and take caution but, once again, put the blame on the car. Finally, consider driving on a clear, sunny day, on a modern highway with no other traffic in sight. The car can respond with agility and promptness: now we would believe the responses to be entirely due to the car itself.

All these environmental variables would have a desirable impact upon the driver's responses, but in a manner attributed to the environment, not the automobile. This would naturally induce just the correct behavior: the more dangerous something appears to be, the more care the person in charge will exert.

Why do we need this? Because the modern automobile has become too comfortable. Between the effective shock absorbers and ride-control systems, effective noise reduction, and minimization of road feel and vibration from the interior of the automobile, the driver is no longer in direct touch with the environment. As a result, artificial enhancement is required, the better to let the driver know the environmental conditions.

Note that I am not in favor of actually making things more dangerous. The goal is that by providing appropriate feedback, the driver will drive more safely. Of course, we should continue to enhance true physical safety. We know that completely automatic systems have already been proven effective: for example, antiskid brakes and stability controls, smoke alarms, helmets for bicyclists and skateboarders and skiers, as well as shields and guards for machinery, are all important. Yet, these automatic systems have limited effectiveness. If drivers drove more safely in the first place, then the automatic systems would be a lot more effective when the unexpected did occur.

These ideas are controversial. Even I am not completely convinced they would work. Human nature being what it is, people are very apt to do just the opposite of my predictions, ignoring the apparent slipperiness of the road by thinking, "Oh, the road isn't really slippery. This is just the car trying to slow me down." But what if the road really is slippery? Furthermore, would you buy a car or tool that deliberately frightened you? Bad marketing strategy. Bad idea.

Still, there is truth in the phenomenon. Today, we are too comfortable, too insulated from the dangers inherent in the world, inherent in the operation of complex, powerful machinery. If motorcycles and automobiles, machinery and drugs seemed as dangerous as they really are, perhaps people would modify their behavior appropriately. When everything is soundproofed, cushioned, and sanitized, we are no longer aware of the real hazards. That is why we need to bring back the truthful depiction of the danger.

Responsive Automation

Power-assisted devices, such as brakes and steering, are relatively primitive examples of a natural collaboration between person and machine. With modern electronics, much more collaboration is possible. Consider the "Cobot," or "Collaborative Robot," invented by Professors Ed Colgate and Michael Peshkin at their Laboratory for Intelligent Mechanical Systems at Northwestern University. Cobots are another excellent example of a natural interaction between a person and a machine, akin to the interaction between a horse and rider. When I asked Peshkin to describe Cobots, here is how he responded:

> The smartest things are those that complement human intelligence, rather than try to supersede it. Much like the smartest teacher.
>
> The point of the Cobot is shared control and shared intelligence between the person and the device. The robot does what it does well, and the person what people do well.
>
> Our first applications are in material handling, in automobile assembly and warehousing. Here the Cobot provides smooth guiding surfaces that the human can use to help move a payload quickly and accurately and more ergonomically. When the payload is not in contact with a virtual surface, the human can move the payload at will, applying vision, dexterity, problem solving skills. And when necessary, push it up against a guiding surface and swoop along it.

The Cobot provides an excellent example of human-machine symbiosis because, as far as the people who use it are concerned, they are simply lifting and moving objects as they normally would. The only difference is that these objects might be extremely heavy; yet, only small lifting and guiding forces are required. The system amplifies force: people only need to exert small, comfortable amounts of force, and the system supplies whatever else is required. The people feel as if they are in complete control and may even be unaware that they are being assisted by mechanical means. For example, one application of Cobot technology helps automobile assembly line workers manipulate automobile engines. Normally, heavy objects, such as automobile engines, are lifted by overhead hoists that must be controlled or by intelligent hoists that try to do the task by themselves automatically. With the Cobot, workers simply loop a chain and hook around the engine and lift up. The engine is far heavier than one person can lift, let alone with one hand, but the Cobot, sensing the lifting action, supplies the lifting force that is required. When workers want the engine to move, or to rotate, or to be lowered again, they simply lift, rotate, push, or press down; the Cobot senses the forces and amplifies them appropriately for the task. The result is a perfect collaboration. The workers do not think of themselves as using a machine: they just think of themselves as moving the engine.

Cobots can be a lot more sophisticated, too. For example, if it is important not to move the engine in some directions, or if it is important to carry the engine along a well-described path, the Cobot control system can define virtual walls and paths so that when the user tries to go against the wall or deviate from the path, the device "pushes back," resisting the attempt, but still in a nice, natural manner. In fact, the worker can use this artificial wall as an aid, pushing the engine all the way to the side until it hits the "wall," then sliding the engine along the wall. Artificially induced limits of this sort feel amazingly natural. The machine doesn't seem to be forcing a behavior: it feels like a physical wall, and so it is natural either to avoid it or perhaps to use it as an aid in maintaining a straight path by deliberately contacting it and sliding along it. Here is how the originators of Cobots described this possibility:

> One of the most exciting capabilities . . . is the implementation of programmable constraint. For example, hard walls which constrain motion to useful directions can dramatically improve performance in tasks such as remote peg-in-hole insertion. Another example . . . [is] the "Magic Mouse," a computer interface device which can constrain an operator's hand to useful directions . . . to avoid, for instance, "slipping off" a pull-down menu. A third example is a robotic surgery system in which a robot positions a guide for a tool held by a surgeon, and a fourth is automobile assembly in which programmed constraints can help an operator navigate large components (e.g., instrument panels, spare tires, seats, doors) into place without collisions.

Cobots are part of a family of power-assisted systems. One other example is that of a powered exoskeleton, a type of suit or mechanical skeleton put on over the body that, just as the

Cobot, senses the person's movements and amplifies them to whatever degree necessary. Exoskeletons are still more of a concept than reality, but proponents of these future things foresee their use in construction, firefighting, and other dangerous environments, enabling a person to lift heavy loads and jump long distances and heights. They could also be beneficial to medical treatments, allowing impaired patients to have normal strength, while also providing rehabilitation training by gradually increasing the amount of force the patient is required to supply, thereby guiding the rehabilitation process. Much like the use of the horse metaphor for automobile control, which can vary between loose rein and tight rein, medical rehabilitation exoskeletons could vary between having the patient in charge (tight rein) and having the robot in charge (loose rein).

Another example of natural interaction is the Segway Personal Transporter, a two-wheeled personal transportation system. The transporter provides a powerful example of how intelligent design can yield a vehicle that is a wonderful symbiosis of machine+person. The transporter provides behavioral control and the human, high-level reflective guidance. Stand on the transporter, and it automatically balances you and it, together. Lean forward, and it moves forward; lean back, and it stops. Similarly, to turn, just lean in the correct direction. It's easier to use than a bicycle, and the interaction feels natural. The Segway transporter isn't for everyone, however, just as a horse isn't for everyone. It requires some degree of skill and attentiveness.

Contrast the natural interaction of horse and rider, person and Cobot, or person and the Segway Transporter with the more

FIGURE 3.4

The Segway® Personal Transporter. A kind of collaborative robot, where control is done by leaning in one direction or another. Naturally, easily, both human and the transporter form a symbiotic unit.

(Photo used with permission of Segway Media.)

rigid interaction between a person and the automatic flight control of an airplane or even the cruise control of an automobile. In the latter, the designers assume that you deliberately set the control, turn it on, and then have nothing more to do—until it fails, that is, when you are suddenly asked to recover from whatever problem has overwhelmed the automation.

The examples of natural, responsive interaction discussed in this section illustrate a natural application of machine intelligence and collaborative power to provide a true machine+person symbiosis—human-machine interaction at its best.

CHAPTER FOUR

Servants of Our Machines

MOTORIST TRAPPED IN TRAFFIC
CIRCLE 14 HOURS

April 1. Hampstead, MA. Motorist Peter Newone said he felt as if a nightmare had just ended. Newone, 53, was driving his newly purchased luxury car when he entered the traffic circle in the city center around 9 a.m. yesterday, Friday. The car was equipped with the latest safety features, including a new feature called Lane Keeping. "It just wouldn't let me get out of the circle," said Newone. "I was in the inner-most lane, and every time I tried to get out, the steering wheel refused to budge and a voice kept saying over and over, 'warning, right lane is occupied.' I was there until 11 at night, when it finally let me out," Newone said from his hospital bed, his voice still shaky. "I managed to get out of the circle and to the side of the road, and then I don't remember what happened."

Police say they found Newone collapsed in his car, incoherent. He was taken to the Memorial Hospital for observation and diagnosed with extreme shock and dehydration. He was released early this morning.

A representative of the automobile company said that they could not explain this behavior. "Our cars are very carefully tested," said Mr. Namron, "and this feature has been most thoroughly vetted by our technicians. It is an essential safety feature and it is designed so that it never exerts more than 80% of the torque required, so the driver can always overrule the system. We designed it that way as a safety precaution. We grieve for Mr. Newone, but we are asking our physicians to do their own evaluation of his condition."

Police say they have never heard of a similar situation. Mr. Newone evidently encountered a rare occurrence of continual traffic at that location: there was a special ceremony in the local school system which kept traffic high all day, and then there was an unusual combination of sports events, a football game, and then a late concert, so traffic was unusually heavy all day and evening. Attempts to get statements from relevant government officials were unsuccessful. The National Transportation Safety Board, which is supposed to investigate all unusual automobile incidents, says that this is not officially an accident, so it does not fit into their domain. Federal and state transportation officials were not available for comment.

Cautious cars, cantankerous kitchens, demanding devices. Cautious cars? We already have them, cautious and sometimes

frightened. Cantankerous kitchens? Not yet, but they are coming. Demanding devices? Oh, yes, our products are getting
smarter, more intelligent, and more demanding, or, if you like,
bossy. This trend brings with it many special problems and un-
explored areas of applied psychology. In particular, our devices
are now part of a human-machine social ecosystem, and therefore they need social graces, superior communicative skills, and
even emotions—machine emotions, to be sure, but emotions
nonetheless.

If you think that the technologies in your home are too complex, too difficult to use, just wait until you see what the next
generation brings: bossy, demanding technologies, technologies
that not only take control of your life but blame you for their
shortcomings. It is tempting to fill this book with horror stories, real ones that are happening today plus imagined ones that
could conceivably come about if current trends continue, such
as the imaginary story of Mr. Newone.

Consider poor Mr. Newone, stuck in the traffic circle for
fourteen hours. Could this really happen? The only real clue
that the story isn't true is the date, April 1, because I wrote this
story specifically for the yearly April Fool's edition of the RISKS
digest, an electronic newsletter devoted to the study of accidents
and errors in the world of high technology. The technologies
described in the article are real, already available on commer-
cially sold automobiles. In theory, just as the spokesperson in
the story says, they only provide 80 percent of the torque required to stay in the lane, so Mr. Newone presumably could
have overcome that force easily. Suppose he were unusually
timid, however, and as soon as he felt the resisting force on the

steering wheel, he would immediately give in. Or what if there were some error in the mechanics, electronics, or programming of the system, causing 100 percent of the force to be deployed, not 80 percent. Could that happen? Who knows, but the fact that it is so plausible is worrisome.

We Have Become the Tools of Our Tools

> But lo! men have become the tools of their tools.
>
> —Henry Thoreau, *Walden*

When Henry Thoreau wrote that "men have become the tools of their tools," he was referring to the relatively simple tools of the 1850s, such as the axe, farming implements, and carpentry. Even in his time, however, tools defined people's lives. "I see young men, my townsmen, whose misfortune it is to have inherited farms, houses, barns, cattle, and farming tools; for these are more easily acquired than got rid of." Today, we complain about the maintenance all our technology requires, for it seems never ending. Thoreau would have sympathized, for even in 1854 he compared the daily toil of his neighbors unfavorably to the twelve labors of Hercules: "The twelve labors of Hercules were trifling in comparison with those which my neighbors have undertaken; for they were only twelve, and had an end."

Today, I would rephrase Thoreau's lament as "People have become slaves to their technology, servants of their tools." The sentiment is the same. And not only must we serve our tools, faithfully using them throughout the day, maintaining them, polishing them, comforting them, but we also blithely follow their prescriptions, even when they lead us to disaster.

It's too late to go back: we can no longer live without the tools of technology. Technology is often blamed as the culprit: "technology is confusing and frustrating," goes the standard cry. Yet, the complaint is misguided: most of our technology works well, including the tool Thoreau was using to write his complaint. For that matter, Thoreau himself was a technologist, a maker of tools, for he helped improve the technology in the manufacture of pencils for his family's pencil business. Yes, a pencil is a technology.

> Tech·nol·o·gy (*noun*): New stuff that doesn't work very
> well or that works in mysterious, unknown ways.

In the common vernacular, the word "technology" is mostly applied to the new things in our life, especially those that are exotic or weird, mysterious or intimidating. Being impressive helps. A rocket ship, surgical robots, the internet—that's technology. But a paper and pencil? Clothes? Cooking utensils? Contrary to the folk definition, the term *technology* really refers to any systematic application of knowledge to fashion the artifacts, materials, and procedures of our lives. It applies to any artificial tool or method. So, our clothing is the result of technology, as is our written language, much of our culture; even music and art can be thought of as either technologies or products that could not exist without the technologies of musical instruments, drawing surfaces, paints, brushes, pencils, and other tools of the artists and musicians.

Until recently, technology has been pretty much under control. Even as technology gained more intelligence, it was still an intelligence that could be understood. After all, people devised it, and people exerted control: starting, stopping, aiming, and directing.

No longer. Automation has taken over many tasks, some thankless—consider the automated equipment that keeps our sewers running properly—and some not so thankless—think of the automated teller machines that put many bank clerks out of work. These automated activities raise major issues for society. Important though this might be, however, my focus here is on those situations where the automation doesn't quite take over, where people are left to pick up the pieces when the automation fails. This is where major stresses occur and where the major dangers, accidents, and deaths result.

Consider the automobile, which, as the *New York Times* notes, "has become a computer on wheels." What is all that computer power being used for? Everything. Controlling the heating and air conditioning with separate controls for the driver and each passenger. Controlling the entertainment system, with a separate audio and video channel for each passenger, including high-definition display screens and surround sound. Communication systems for telephone, text messaging, e-mail. Navigation systems that tell you where you are, where you are going, what the traffic conditions are, where the closest restaurants, gas stations, hotels, and entertainment spots are located, and paying for road tolls, drive-through restaurants, and downloaded movies and music.

Much of the automation, of course, is used to control the car. Some things are completely automated, so the driver and passengers are completely unaware of them: the timing of critical events such as spark, valve opening and closing, fuel injection, engine cooling, power-assisted brakes and steering. Some of the automation, including braking and stability systems, is partially controllable and noticeable. Some of the technology interacts with the driver: navigational systems, cruise control, lane-keeping systems, even automatic parking. And this barely scratches the surface of what exists today, and what is planned for the future.

Precrash warning systems now use their forward-looking radar to predict when the automobile is apt to get into a crash, preparing themselves for the eventuality. Seats straighten up, seat belts tighten, and the brakes get ready. Some cars have television cameras that monitor the driver, and if the driver does not appear to be looking straight ahead, they warn the driver with lights and buzzers. If the driver still fails to respond, they apply the brakes automatically. Someday, we might imagine the following interchange at a court trial:

> **Prosecutor:** "I now call the next witness. Mr. Automobile, is it your sworn testimony that just before the crash the defendant was not watching the road?"
>
> **Automobile:** "Correct. He was looking to his right the whole time, even after I signaled and warned him of the danger."
>
> **Prosecutor:** "And what did the defendant try to do to you?"
>
> **Automobile:** "He tried to erase my memory, but I have an encrypted, tamper-proof storage system."

Your car will soon chat with neighboring cars, exchanging all sorts of interesting information. Cars will communicate with one another through wireless networks, technically called "ad hoc" networks because they form as needed, letting them warn one another about what's down the road. Just as automobiles and trucks from the oncoming lane sometimes warn you of police vehicles by flashing their lights (or sending messages over their two-way radios and cell phones), future automobiles will tell oncoming autos about traffic and highway conditions, obstacles, collisions, bad weather, and all sorts of other things, some useful, some not, while simultaneously learning about what they can expect to encounter. Cars may even exchange more than that, including information the inhabitants might consider personal and private.

Gossiping cars. When two cars talk to one another, what do they talk about? Why, the weather, or traffic patterns, or how to negotiate the intersection they are both approaching at high speed. At least, that's what the researchers are working on. But you can also bet that clever advertisers are thinking about the potential. Each billboard can have its own wireless network, broadcasting its wares to the car. Imagine a billboard or store checking with the navigation system to see just what the car's destination is, perhaps to suggest a restaurant, hotel, or shopping center. What if it could take control of the navigation system, reprogramming it to instruct the driver to turn into the advertiser's establishment? When the day comes that the steering is under the car's control, the car might very well decide to take you to the restaurant of its choice, possibly even preordering your favorite food for you. "What," the car might say to you,

"you mean you don't want your favorite food every day, every meal? Strange—why is it your favorite, then?"

What about an overload of advertisements or viruses inserted into the telephones, computers, and navigation system in the auto? Is this possible? Never underestimate the cleverness of advertisers, or mischief makers, or criminals. Once systems are networked together, it is amazing what unexpected events can transpire. The technology experts say it is not a matter of if but of when. It is always a race, and no matter what the good guys do, the bad guys always figure out a way to wreak havoc.

Hitting the Conference Circuit

Old MacDonald had a conference, ee-eye, ee-eye oh. Here a conference, there a conference, everywhere a conference.

One nice thing about academic life: there are always conferences in exotic locations. Florence in the summer, Hyderabad in the winter (but certainly never in the summer). Stanford in the spring, Daejon in the fall. There is a large industry in providing exotic conference centers.

The conferences and centers are not just for show: real work actually gets accomplished. The money sometimes comes from governmental granting agencies or foundations, sometimes from organizations such as the United Nations or the North Atlantic Treaty Organization, sometimes from private industry. Whatever the source of the funds, the grantors keep a strict eye out for results—positive, substantive results, like books, research reports, inventions, devices, desired breakthroughs. Of course, this guarantees that the call for papers will glorify the wonders that will soon result from these expected break-throughs, and the resulting conference reports will be optimistic to a fault. The exceptions, of course, are those conferences run by the humanists and philosophers whose conference call will emphasize the approaching dangers from all these expected breakthroughs.

I find myself invited to events held by both sides—those expecting the technology of the future to free us and those expecting it to degrade and enslave us. My take is to deemphasize both claims. Technology will not set us free. It will never solve all the problems of humankind. Moreover, for all the problems that are solved, new ones will arise. Neither will the technology enslave us, at least not any more than it already does. Once we get used to it, the daily requirements of our technologies do not feel like enslavement. Mostly, they feel like improvements. Most people wash their hands several times a day, bathing frequently, and changing clothes daily. This wasn't the case in earlier eras: is this enslavement? We prepare our meals with cooking and eating utensils made of complex materials, on stoves heated by electricity or gas, produced far away through advanced technological means and transported to our homes through complex networks of pipes and wires. Is this enslavement? Not to me.

I believe that the new technologies will mainly befuddle and confuse, frustrate and annoy us, even while delivering some of the promised benefits. After deployment, technologies always deliver benefits never contemplated by their designers and developers, along with problems and difficulties never conceived of.

There is many a cry that we should not release new technologies into the world until we have thought through all the benefits and disadvantages, carefully weighing the one against the other. Sounds good. Alas, it is quite impossible. The unexpected consequences of technologies always outweigh the expected ones, both the positive and the negative. And if they are unexpected, how can we plan for them?

Want to know what the future will be about? Keep an eye on those conferences. Nothing is going to happen in the future, not in technology anyway, without huge early-warning signs in the research laboratories of the world, all duly announced in the scientific journals, at a host of conferences, and through the establishment of centers for research. It usually takes a long time, decades, for ideas to move from conception to product, and that time is engaged in continual interaction with others pursuing similar ideas. Along the way, industrial forces take sufficient interest that the work starts to become commercialized, at which point it becomes invisible, hidden inside corporate research and development centers, carefully guarded.

Beyond those locked doors, however, there is the public world of conferences. And there a lot is going on, all under many labels: assistance, smart, and intelligent; ubiquitous computers, invisible ones, or perhaps ones still in the process of disappearing; ambient technologies intended to fit seamlessly into a life, but only if the life itself has been altered to make the seams invisible. Here are selected quotations from two conference announcements, just so you get the drift:

INTERACTION CHALLENGES FOR INTELLIGENT
ASSISTANTS, STANFORD UNIVERSITY, CA, USA
In an increasingly complex world, a new wave of intelligent artificial assistants has the potential to simplify and amplify our everyday personal and professional lives.

These assistants will help us in mundane tasks from purchasing groceries to organizing meetings; in background tasks from providing reminders to monitoring our health; and in complex, open-ended tasks from writing a report to locating survivors in a collapsed building.

Some will offer tutelage or provide recommendations. Whether robotic embodiments or software processes, these assistive agents will help us manage our time and budgets, knowledge and workflow as they assist us in our homes, offices, cars, and public spaces.

INTERNATIONAL WORKSHOP ON ARTIFICIAL INTELLIGENCE (AI) FOR HUMAN COMPUTING. HYDERABAD, INDIA, JANUARY

Human Computing is about next-generation anticipatory interfaces that should be about humans, built for humans, and based on models of humans. They should go beyond the traditional keyboard and mouse to include natural, human-like interactive functions, including understanding and emulating behavioral and social signaling.

"Humanlike interactive functions": the very phrase suggests secretive, mysterious nonbeings out to do our bidding. Socially assistive robots that will teach, entertain, and safeguard our children and entertain and safeguard our elderly (presumably, they no longer need teaching), ensuring that they take their medicine, don't do dangerous activities, and if they fall down, either the robots will help them up or, at least, call for help.

Yes, the development of intelligent devices that can read our minds, cater to all our wishes (even before we are aware of them), and take care of the young, the elderly, the hospitalized, and even the rest of us, is a growing industry. Robots to talk with you, robots to cook for you, robots this and robots that. "Smart home" research projects show up all over the world.

The reality is a lot less than the dreams. Artificially intelligent agents are the mainstay of many a computer game, but that doesn't count as real assistance in everyday lives. And yes, the technology behind the ever popular line of robotic vacuum cleaners can be expanded indefinitely to all tasks that simply require navigating over a designated area with sufficient thoroughness: cleaning a swimming pool, sweeping leaves from a yard or mowing the grass. The reality is that intelligent devices can indeed interact well with the physical world or other intelligent devices. It is when they must interact with real people that the difficulties begin.

Intelligent devices do work well in controlled settings where the task is well specified, such as washing clothes. They also are very effective in industrial settings, where not only is the task well specified, but the people who control and supervise them are well trained, spending hours learning how the devices work, often spending considerable time in simulators, where many of the failures can be experienced and appropriate responses learned. But there are profound differences between intelligent devices in industrial settings and the very same technologies in the home. First, the technologies are apt to be different, for although industry can afford to spend tens of thousands of dollars on automation, home owners are usually only willing to spend tens or hundreds of dollars. Second, in industrial settings, the people are extremely well trained, whereas in the home and in the automobile, they are relatively untrained. Third, in most industrial settings, when difficulties arise, there is considerable time before damage might be done. In the automobile, the time is measured in seconds.

Intelligent devices have made great progress in the control of automobiles, airplanes, and ships. They make sense for machines with fixed tasks. They work well in the world of computer agents, where they need only some intelligence and an image to display on the screen; real, physical bodies are not needed. They are successful in games and entertainment, controlling dolls, robotic pets, and characters in computer games. In these environments, not only do occasional misunderstandings and failures not matter, but they can add to the fun. In the world of entertainment, a well-executed failure can be even more satisfying than success.

Tools that rely on statistical inference are also widely popular and successful. Some online stores recommend books, movies, music, or even kitchen appliances by finding products that people similar to you in taste seem to like, then recommending those items to you. The system works reasonably well.

Despite the multiple conferences and the well-formed beliefs of scientists throughout the world, making devices that truly interact with us in useful ways is far beyond our capabilities. Why? Oh, for lots of reasons. Some are for physical reasons: devices—or robots—that can go up and down stairs, walk around the natural environment, and pick up, manipulate, and control real, naturally occurring objects are still far beyond our capabilities. Some reasons are lack of knowledge: the science of understanding human behavior is growing rapidly, but even so, what we do not know far exceeds what we do. Our ability to create natural interaction is very limited.

Cars That Drive Themselves, Houses That Clean Themselves, Entertainment Systems That Decide How You Shall Be Entertained

What's next? Clearly, we are headed for cars that drive themselves; washing machines that determine the color and material of clothes, adjusting themselves automatically; cooking appliances that mix, heat, and stir, making the entire meal, after selecting the foods you should eat, having collaborated with the refrigerator and your medical records. Entertainment systems will select your music for you and prerecord television shows and movies they determine might be of interest, automatically deducting the charges from your bank account. Houses will take care of the temperature settings, of watering the lawn. Robot cleaners and lawn mowers will vacuum, mop, dust, and, of course, mow the lawn. Much of this has already happened. Most of this will soon happen.

Of all the areas of automation that impact our everyday lives, the most advanced is that of the automobile. So, let's take a quick look at what is happening here, although the level of automation required to give the family vehicle full driving capability still remains far in the future. Some people estimate it will take twenty to fifty years, and chances are that this estimate will still be accurate no matter when you read this. In some circumstances, cars can—and already do—drive themselves.

How do we automate sensibly, controlling some parts of the driving experience but ensuring that drivers are kept alert and informed? "In the loop," is the way this is described in aviation safety. How do we warn drivers who are about to change lanes that there is another vehicle in the way, or that there is an obstacle in the road or a car approaching from an intersecting side street, which is not yet visible to the driver?

What should be done when two cars arrive at an intersection on a collision course, and one car decides the best way to avoid a crash is to accelerate past the danger zone at the same time as the driver decides the best solution is to brake? Should the car ignore the pressure on the brake pedal and just accelerate? Should a car prevent its driver from changing lanes when another vehicle is in the other lane? Should the car prevent the driver from exceeding the speed limit, or from going slower than the minimum limit, or from getting too close to the car ahead? All of these questions and more face automobile engineers and designers today. In many of these situations, asking the driver what to do, or even giving the driver the relevant information, is seldom possible: there simply isn't enough time.

Cars today can almost drive themselves. Take adaptive cruise control, which adjusts the auto's speed according to its distance from the car in front. Add lane-keeping control and automatic toll-payment systems, and the car can drive itself, following the roadway and debiting the driver's bank account. Lane keeping is not (yet) completely reliable, and in chapter 1, I discussed some of the problems with adaptive cruise control, but these systems will improve in reliability and be available at greatly lowered costs, so that they will eventually be installed in all car models. When cars start communicating among themselves (something that is already happening in experimental deployment), safety will increase even more. The technology does not have to be perfect to improve safety: human drivers are far from perfect.

Put all these components together, and, oops, we are training drivers to be inattentive. Their cars will be able to drive on highways for hours with little need for driver interaction: the driver could even fall asleep. This already happens in aviation: the automatic pilots are so good that pilots have indeed fallen asleep. A friend, a physicist who worked for a navy research laboratory, once told me that he was in an airplane doing experiments for the navy, flying over the ocean for several hours. When the tests were finished, his group called the cockpit to tell the pilots. There was no response, so they went forward to talk to them: the pilots were asleep.

Falling asleep isn't recommended for airplane pilots, but it is usually safe because of the efficiency of the automatic flight controls, especially when flying in an uncrowded air space, with good weather, and with plenty of fuel. This is not the case for automobile drivers. Studies have shown that the chance of accident increases severely if the driver's eyes are away from the road for more than two seconds. And the driver doesn't have to be asleep: two seconds looking away from the road or fiddling with the radio is enough.

In many of the classical fields studied by engineering psychologists and human factors engineers, there is a well-known and well-studied problem called *overautomation*: the equipment is so good that people don't need to be as attentive. In theory, people are supposed to supervise the automation, always watching over operations, always ready to step in if things go wrong, but this kind of supervision is very difficult when the automation works so well. In the case of some manufacturing or process control plants, there may be very little for the human operators to do for days. As a result, people simply cannot maintain their attention.

Swarms and Platoons

Birds flock, bees swarm, and fish school. They are fun to watch, moving in precise formation, swooping here, banking there, splitting up to avoid obstacles, smoothly rejoining on the other side. It is precision action; they move in synchrony, close to one another, all obeying the leader precisely, immediately, without collision.

Except there is no leader. Swarming behavior, as well as its analog among flocks of birds, schools of fish, and stampeding herds of cattle, results when each animal obeys a remarkably simple set of behavioral rules. Each individual creature avoids collisions with the other animals and objects that might be in its path, tries to keep close to all of the others—without touching them, of course—and keeps moving in the same direction as its neighbors. Communication within the swarm, school, or flock is limited to perceptual information: sight, sound, pressure waves (e.g., lateral-line detectors in fish) and smell (e.g., in ants).

In artificial systems, we can use more informative communication. Suppose we had a group of automobiles traveling down a highway, connected through a wireless communication network. Aha! The cars could actually travel in a swarm. Natural, biological swarms are reactive: its members react to each other's behavior. Artificial swarms, however, such as a group of cars, can be predictive because cars can communicate their intended behavior, so others can react, even before anything happens.

Imagine a swarm of cars, where each car is completely automatic, communicating with the other cars in the vicinity. They could cruise down the highway rapidly and safely. They wouldn't have to keep much separation between themselves either—a few feet or a meter would do. If the lead car intended to slow or brake, it could tell the others, and within thousandths of a second, they would slow down or brake as well. With human drivers, we must keep a large separation to give people time to react and decide what to do: with automatic swarms, the time to react is measured in milliseconds.

With swarms, we wouldn't need traffic lanes. After all, these are needed only to help drivers avoid collision. Swarms don't collide, so no lanes are required. We wouldn't need traffic lanes, stop signs, or traffic lights, either. At an intersection, the swarm would simply follow its rules to avoid crashing into crossing traffic. Each car would adjust its speed and position, some slowing, some speeding, so intersecting streams of traffic would magically cross one another, with no car ever hitting another. For this, the swarm rules would have to be modified somewhat to make sure that a car on a cross street wouldn't start following its new neighbor instead of its original ones, but that wouldn't be hard to do.

What about pedestrians? In theory, the rule of avoiding collisions would work here as well. A pedestrian would simply walk across the street. The swarming vehicles would slow, speed, and swerve, just enough so as always to leave a clear space for the pedestrian. It would be a rather terrifying experience, requiring incredible trust on the pedestrian's part, but in theory it could be done.

What if a car needed to leave the swarm or to go to a destination different from that of its swarm mates? The driver would tell his or her car of this intention, and the car would in turn communicate it to the other vehicles. Or the driver would use the turn signal to tell the car of the wish to change lanes, and the car would inform all the neighboring vehicles. To get into the lane on the right, the car just ahead in the right lane would speed up slightly, the one just behind in the right lane would slow down slightly, making space. Tapping the brake pedal would signal the intention to slow down or stop, and the other cars would get out of the way.

Different swarms might even share information. Thus, a swarm going in one direction might share information with a swarm going in the other direction, giving it useful information about what might lie ahead. Alternatively, if the density of vehicles were high enough, information might trickle backwards from the lead car to those behind, telling the following vehicles of accidents, traffic, or other relevant driving information.

Swarms are still the stuff of research laboratories. Instituting swarmlike behavior in real cars creates major challenges. One is understanding how this could work when not all cars will be equipped with the wireless communication equipment that is required for swarming. Another is figuring out how to handle the many varieties of automobiles on the road, some with fully automatic control and wireless communication equipment, some with outdated equipment, and some with no equipment at all or with malfunctioning equipment. Would the cars have to figure out who was the least capable in the bunch and then all revert to that behavior? Nobody has answers to these questions.

And there is more. Suppose an antisocial driver came upon a swarm filling up all the space on the road. If the antisocial car preferred to go at a much faster speed, it would only have to accelerate and drive straight through the swarm, confident that all the other cars would automatically get out of the way. This would work fine for one discrepant vehicle but could lead to disaster if others were doing the same thing at the same time.

Not all vehicles will have the same abilities. When some cars are still driven manually, we will need to consider realistic driver behavior, due to mixed levels of skill or mixed levels of attentiveness, drowsiness, or distraction. Heavy trucks have slower response times and longer stopping distances than cars. Different cars have a wide variety of stopping, acceleration, and turning capabilities.

Despite the drawbacks, swarming has lots of benefits. Because swarming cars can travel very closely to one another, more cars can fit on a given highway, relieving traffic considerably. Moreover, normal traffic slows down as the density increases: swarms would not have to slow down until the density reached far higher levels. Cars traveling close together help reduce wind resistance. (This is why bicycle racers cluster together: the "drafting" behavior of bikers reduces air resistance.) Even so, don't expect to see swarms for quite awhile.

Platoons, now that is another story. A platoon is a simplified swarm, working in one dimension. In a platoon, one vehicle follows the one just in front, mimicking its speed precisely. When a sequence of cars travels in a platoon, a driver is only needed for the first vehicle: the others just tag along. Some of the swarm benefits apply here as well: increased density of traffic and reduced energy through drafting. Experimental studies, some done on public highways, show a dramatic increase in traffic capacity for a given highway. Platoons, like swarms, face the most difficulty when drivers enter or exit and when there are mixed-mode cars, and some with and, some without automatic communication capability. Of course, drivers who wish to exploit the system or simply to cause disruption can do so, both in platoons and swarms.

Platoons and swarms are only a few of the many forms of automation now being considered for the modern automobile. Platooning, in fact, comes free with some forms of adaptive cruise control. After all, if the cruise control can slow the vehicle's speed when a car moves in front, then the car automatically will track the car in front as it changes speed, as long as it stays under the speed set into the cruise control. In heavy traffic, the car will follow the one in front closely, increasing separation as speed increases. For a fully automatic system, the separation between the two cars could be small, with no need to increase the distance by much as speed increased. Without people in control, the traffic would flow much more smoothly and efficiently, that is, as long as everything worked perfectly, as long as no unexpected events occurred.

Efficient platooning cannot be done without fully automatic braking, steering, and speed control. Moreover, it requires a guaranteed high-degree of reliability—perfect reliability some would say, reliability so high that it would never be questioned. As with swarms, however, it is not at all obvious how such platooning could be introduced into the existing highway system, given that we already have a huge number of vehicles incapable of platooning. How would we separate the automated from the nonautomated ones? How would a driver enter or exit the platoon? What if something went wrong?

Swarming works just fine in the laboratory, but it is difficult to imagine on the highway. Platooning may be more feasible. I can imagine special lanes restricted to platooning cars, perhaps enforcing an equipment check on the communication and control capabilities of each vehicle before it is allowed into the platoon. Platooning will speed traffic and reduce congestion while also saving fuel. Sounds like a winning proposition. The complexity, of course, comes in the transition: getting cars safely into and out of the platoon and enforcing the equipment requirements.

The Problem of Inappropriate Automation

I once argued that the current state of automation was fundamentally unsound because it was in the dangerous middle ground, neither fully automated nor fully manual. Either have no automation or full automation, I argued, but what we have today is halfway automation. Even worse, the system takes over when the going is easy and gives up, usually without any warning, when the going gets tough—just the reverse of what you would want.

If an airplane pilot or car driver is aware of the vehicle's state, the environment, and the location and condition of all other vehicles and, moreover, is continually reacting and interpreting this information, the person is an essential part of the control loop: perceiving the situation, deciding upon an appropriate action to take, executing that action, and then monitoring the result. You are "in the loop" every time you drive your car with care, paying full attention to all that is happening around you. For that matter, you are in the loop while cooking, washing, or even playing a video game, as long as you are continually involved in judging the situation, deciding what to do, and evaluating the result.

A closely related concept is that of *situation awareness*, which refers to a person's knowledge of the context, the current state of things, and what might happen next. In theory, a person could still be in the loop, stay fully aware of the situation, even with completely automated equipment, by continually monitoring the vehicle's actions and assessing the situation, being ready to step in when needed. This passive observation is not very rewarding, however, especially as airplane pilots and automobile drivers might have to maintain this state for many hours on long-distance trips. In experimental psychology, this situation is often called *vigilance*, and the experimental and theoretical studies of vigilance demonstrate deterioration in performance with time. People just can't keep focused on mindless tasks for very long.

When people are "out of the loop," they are no longer informed. If something goes wrong and immediate response is required, they cannot provide it effectively. Instead, considerable time and effort is required to get back "into the loop," and by then, it may be too late.

A second problem with automated equipment is the tendency to rely on the automation, even when there are difficulties with it. Two British psychologists, Neville Stanton and Mark Young of Brunel University, studied drivers using adaptive cruise control in an automobile simulator. They found that when the automation worked, things were fine, but when the adaptive cruise control failed, the drivers had more accidents than did drivers without the fancy technology. This is a common finding: safety equipment does indeed increase safety, until it fails. When people learn to rely upon automation, they are not only out of the loop but often too trusting of the automation. When it fails, they are less likely to catch problems than they would be if they didn't have automated equipment at all. This phenomenon has been found in every domain studied, be it among airline pilots, train operators, or automobile drivers.

This tendency to follow instructions provided by automated equipment has its bizarre side as well. The residents of Wiltshire, England, have discovered a lucrative business: towing automobiles out of the River Avon, after drivers have followed the instructions of their navigation systems, even though common sense should have told them they were about to drive into a river. Similarly, even experienced airline pilots sometimes trust their equipment more than they should. The cruise ship *Royal Majesty* went aground because its crew had too much faith in its intelligent navigation system.

All automobile manufacturers are concerned about these issues. In addition to addressing actual safety in this modern, litigious society, they worry that even the slightest problem may cause massive lawsuits against them. So, how do they respond? Cautiously, very cautiously.

Driving a vehicle at high speeds over crowded highways is hazardous: there are over 1.2 million deaths and 50 million injuries each year in the world. This is truly a situation where our reliance on a machine, the automobile, exposes all of us to unnecessary risk—one that is helpful, invaluable to the population of the world, and deadly.

Yes, we could train drivers better, but part of the problem is that driving is inherently dangerous. When problems arise, they do so quickly, with little time to respond. Every driver experiences wavering levels of attention—a natural human condition. Even in the best of cases, driving is a dangerous activity.

If one cannot automate fully, then the automation that is possible must be applied with great care, sometimes not being invoked, sometimes requiring more human participation than is really needed in order to keep the human drivers informed and attentive. Full manual control of automobiles is dangerous. Fully automatic control will be safer. The difficulty lies in the transition toward full automation, when only some things will be automated, when different vehicles will have different capabilities, and when even the automation that is installed will be limited in capability. I fear that while the partial automation of driving will lead to fewer accidents, the accidents that do happen will be greater in magnitude, involve more cars, and exact a higher toll. The joint relationship between machines and their humans must be approached with caution.

CHAPTER FIVE

The Role of Automation

Why do we need automation? Many technologists cite three major reasons: to eliminate the dull, the dangerous, and the dirty. It is difficult to argue with this answer, but many things are automated for other reasons—to simplify a complex task, to reduce the work force, to entertain—or simply because it can be done.

Even successful automation always comes at a price, for in the process of taking over one set of tasks, it invariably introduces a new set of issues. Automation often satisfactorily performs its task but adds an increased need for maintenance. Some automation exchanges the need for skilled laborers with the need for caretakers. In general, whenever any task is automated, the impact is felt far beyond the one task. Rather, the application of automation is a system issue, changing the way work is done, restructuring jobs, shifting the required tasks from one portion of the population to another, and, in many cases, eliminating the need for some functions and adding the need for others. For some people, automation is helpful; for

others, especially those whose jobs have been changed or elimi-
nated, it can be terrible.

The automation of even simple tasks has an impact. Consider the mundane task of making a cup of coffee. I use an automated machine that makes coffee at the push of a button,
automatically heating the water, grinding the beans, brewing
the coffee, and disposing of the grounds. The result is that I
have replaced the mild tedium of making coffee each morning
with the more onerous need to maintain my machine. The water and bean containers must be filled, the inner parts of the
machine must be disassembled and cleaned periodically, and all
areas in contact with liquid must be cleaned both of coffee
residue and calcium deposits (then the machine must be
cleaned again to remove all vestiges of the cleaning solution
used to dissolve the calcium deposits). Why all this effort to
minimize the difficulty of a task that isn't really very difficult in
the first place? The answer, in this case, is that the automation
allows me to time-shift the demand on my attention: I trade a
little bit of work at an inconvenient time—when I have just
awakened, am still somewhat sleepy, in a rush—with considerable work later, which I can schedule to be at my convenience.

The trend toward increasing automation seems unstoppable
in terms of both the sheer number of tasks and activities that
are becoming automated and the intelligence and autonomy of
the machines that are taking over these tasks. Automation is not
inevitable, however. Moreover, there is no reason why automation must present us with so many deficiencies and problems. It
should be possible to develop technology that truly minimizes
the dull, the dangerous, and the dirty, without introducing huge
negative side effects.

Smart Things

Smart Homes

It's late in the evening in Boulder, Colorado, and Mike Mozer is sitting in his living room, reading. After a while he yawns, stretches, then stands up and wanders toward his bedroom. The house, ever alert to his activity, decides that he is going to bed, so it turns off the living room lights and turns on the lights in the entry, the master bedroom, and the master bath. It also turns the heat down. Actually, it is the computer system in his house that continually monitors Mozer's behavioral patterns and adjusts the lighting, heating, and other aspects of the home to prepare for his anticipated behavior. This is no ordinary program. It operates through what is called a "neural network" designed to mimic the pattern-recognition and learning abilities of human neurons, thus, the human brain. Not only does it recognize Mozer's activity patterns, but it can appropriately anticipate his behavior most of the time. A neural network is a powerful pattern recognizer, and because it examines the sequence of his activities, including the time of day at which they occur, it predicts both what he will do and when. As a result, when Mozer leaves the house to go to work, it turns off the heat and hot water heater in order to save energy, but when its circuits anticipate his return, it turns them back on again so that the house will be comfortable when he enters.

Is this house smart? Intelligent? The designer of this automated system, Mike Mozer, doesn't think so: he calls it "adaptive." It is instructive to look at Mozer's experience as we try to understand just what it means to be intelligent. The house has over seventy-five sensors that measure each room's temperature, ambient light, sound levels, door and window positions, the weather outside and amount of sunlight, and any movements by inhabitants. Actuators control the heating of the rooms and the hot water, lighting, and ventilation. The system contains more than five miles of cabling. Neural network computer software can learn, so the house is continually adapting its behavior according to Mozer's preferences. If it selects a setting that is not appropriate, Mozer corrects the setting, and the house then changes its behavior. One journalist described how this happens:

> Mozer demonstrated the bathroom light, which turned on to a low intensity as he entered. "The system picks the lowest level of the light or heat it thinks it can get away with in order to conserve energy, and I need to complain if I am not satisfied with its decision," he said. To express his discomfort, he hit a wall switch, causing the system to brighten the light and to "punish itself" so that the next time he enters the room, a higher intensity will be selected.

The house trains its owner as much as the owner trains the house. When working late at night at the university, Mozer would sometimes realize that he had to get home: his house was expecting him, dutifully turning on the heat and hot water, getting ready for his arrival. This raises an interesting question: why can't he just call his home and tell it that he is going to be late? Similarly, his attempt to discover and fix some faulty hardware led to a system that also could detect when someone dawdled too long in the bathroom. "Long after the hardware problem was resolved," said Mozer, "we left the broadcast message in the system, because it provided useful feedback to the inhabitants about how their time was being spent." So, now the house warns inhabitants when they spend too much time in the bathroom? This home sounds like a real nag.

Is this an intelligent house? Here are some more comments by Mozer himself on the limits to the control system's intelligence:

> The Adaptive House project has inspired much brain-storming about ways to extend the project further, most of which seem entirely misguided. One idea often mentioned is controlling home entertainment systems—stereos, TVs, radios, etc. The problem with selection of video and audio in the home is that the inhabitants' preferences will depend on state of mind, and few cues are directly available from the environment—even using machine vision—that correlate with state of mind. The result is likely to be that the system mispredicts often and annoys the inhabitants more than it supports them. The annoyance is magnified by the fact that when inhabitants seek audio or video entertainment, they generally have an explicit intention to do so. This intention contrasts with, say, temperature regulation in a home, where the inhabitants do not consciously consider the temperature unless it becomes uncomfortable. If inhabitants are aware of their goals, achieving the goal is possible with a simple click of a button, and errors—such as blasting the stereo when one is concentrating on a difficult problem—are all but eliminated. The benefit/cost trade-off falls on the side of manual control.

If only the house could read the mind of its owner. It is this inability to read minds, or, as the scientists prefer to say, to infer a person's intentions, that defeats these systems. Here the problem goes far beyond the lack of common ground, as anyone who has ever lived with another person knows. There may be much sharing of knowledge and activities, but it is still difficult to know exactly what another person intends to do. In theory, the mythical British butler could anticipate the wants and desires of his master, although my knowledge of how well this succeeds comes from novels and television—not the most reliable sources. Even here, much of the butler's success comes about because his employers' lives are well regulated by the pace of social events, so that the schedule dictates which tasks need doing.

Automatic systems that decide whether or not to do some activity can, of course, be right or wrong. Failures come in two forms: misses and false alarms. A miss means that the system has failed to detect a situation, therefore to perform the desired action. A false alarm means that the system has acted when it shouldn't have. Think of an automated fire detection system. A miss is a failure to signal a fire when it happens. A false alarm is the signaling of a fire, even though none is present. These two forms of error have different costs.

A failure to detect a fire can have disastrous consequences, but false detections can also create problems. If the only action taken by the fire detector is to sound an alarm, a false alarm is mostly just a nuisance, but it also diminishes trust in the system. But what if the false alarm turns on the sprinkler system and notifies the fire department? Here the cost can be enormous, especially if the water damages valuable objects. If a smart home misreads the intentions of its occupants, the costs of misses and false alarms are usually small. If the music system suddenly comes on because the house thinks the resident would like to hear music, it is annoying but not dangerous. If the system diligently turns up the heat every morning, even though the inhabitants are away on vacation, there are no serious consequences. In an automobile, however, if the driver relies on the car to slow up every time it gets too close to the car in front, a miss can be life threatening. And a false alarm, where the car veers because it thinks the driver is wandering out of his lane or brakes because it incorrectly thinks something is in front of it, can be life threatening if nearby vehicles are surprised by the action and fail to respond quickly enough.

Whether false alarms are dangerous or simply annoying, they diminish trust. After a few false alarms, the alarm system will be disregarded. Then, if there is a real fire, the inhabitants are apt to ignore the warning as "just another false alarm." Trust develops over time and is based on experience, along with continual reliable interaction.

The Mozer home system works for its owner because he is also the scientist who built it, so he is more forgiving of problems. Because he is a research scientist and an expert on neural networks, his home serves as a research laboratory. It is a wonderful experiment and would be great fun to visit, but I don't think I would want to live there.

Homes That Make People Smart

In sharp contrast to the fully automated home that tries to do things automatically, a group of researchers at Microsoft Research Cambridge (England) designs homes with devices that augment human intelligence. Consider the problem of coordinating the activities of a home's inhabitants—say, a family with two working adults and two teenagers. This presents a daunting problem. The technologist's traditional approach in dealing with multiple agendas is to imagine intelligent calendars. For example, the home could match up the schedules of every house member to determine when meals should be scheduled and who should drive others to and from their activities. Just imagine your home continually communicating with you—e-mailing, instant messaging, text messaging, or even telephoning—reminding you of your appointments, when you need to be home for dinner, when to pick up other family members, or even when to stop at the market on the way home.

Before you know it, your home will expand its domain, recommending articles or television shows it thinks might interest you. Is this how you want to lead your life? Many researchers apparently think so. This is the approach followed by most developers of smart homes in research facilities at universities and industrial research laboratories around the world. It is all very efficient, all very modern, and most unhuman.

The research team in Microsoft's Cambridge laboratories started with the premise that people make homes smart, not technology. They decided to support each particular family's solution to their own needs, not to automate any one solution. The team spent time doing what's known as *ethnographic research*, observing home dwellers, watching real, everyday behavior. The goal is not to get in the way, not to change anything that is happening, but to be unobtrusive, simply watching and recording how people go about their normal activities.

A comment about research methods: you probably think that if a crew of scientists showed up at your home with voice recorders, cameras, and video camcorders, they could hardly be considered unobtrusive. In fact, the typical family adapts to experienced researchers and goes about its usual business, including family squabbles and disagreements. This "applied ethnography," or "rapid ethnography," is different from the ethnographic work of anthropologists who spend years in exotic locations carefully observing a group's behavior. When applied scientists, engineers, and designers study the culture of the modern household in order to provide assistance, the goal is first to discover the places where people have difficulties, then to determine things that might aid them in those places. For this purpose, the designers are looking for large phenomena, major points of frustration or annoyance, where simple solutions can have a major, positive effect. This approach has been quite successful.

Family members communicate with one another through a wide variety of means. They write messages and notes that they leave wherever they think they might be noticed—on chairs, desktops, and computer keyboards, pasted on computer screens, or placed on stairs, beds, or doors. Because the kitchen has become the central gathering point for many families, one of the most common places to post notices is on the refrigerator. Most refrigerators are made of steel, and steel affords a hold for magnets. The original discoverers of magnets would be amazed to see that in today's home, the major use of magnets is to affix notes and announcements, children's drawings, and photographs to the front and sides of the refrigerator. This has spawned a small industry that makes refrigerator magnets, clips, notepads, frames for photos and pens, all to be fastened to the doors and sides.

Expensive refrigerators are often made of stainless steel, or the door is covered with wood paneling, thus destroying the affordance: magnets don't stick. When this happened to me, my initial reaction was annoyance to discover that an unintended consequence of the move to wood was the loss of my home communication center. Post-it notes still work but are aesthetically unacceptable on such appliances. Fortunately, entrepreneurs have rushed to fill the void, creating bulletin boards that can be mounted more discretely in the kitchen, and some of these have steel surfaces that provide a receptive home for magnets.

The very popularity of the refrigerator creates a problem, as you can see in Figure 5.1. Too many announcements, photographs, and newspaper clippings make it difficult to tell when a new item has been added. In addition, the refrigerator is not always the most appropriate place for either the note sender or its intended recipient. The Microsoft team developed a series of "augmented" note devices, which included a set of "reminding magnets." One form of magnet glows gently for a period after being moved, drawing people's attention to the notice underneath. Another set of magnets is labeled by the day of the week, each of which glows subtly when the specific day has arrived, attracting attention without being bothersome. Thus, the "garbage pickup is Wednesday morning" magnet can be pinned to the refrigerator with the Tuesday magnet.

The fixed location of the refrigerator was overcome through cellular and internet technology. The team devised the notepad shown in Figure 5.2A. It can be placed in the kitchen adjacent to the refrigerator (or anywhere in the house, for that matter) and

FIGURE 5.1

The refrigerator and "reminding magnets" studied by the Microsoft Research group at Cambridge, England. The top photograph is a typical refrigerator door being used as a bulletin board. When there are so many notes, it is difficult to find the relevant ones. The bottom picture shows the smart magnets: Put the "wednesday" magnet over the note relevant to that day, and when Wednesday comes, the magnet starts glowing, reminding without annoying.

*(Photographs courtesy of the Socio-Digital Systems Group,
Microsoft Research Cambridge)*

allows messages to be added from anywhere through e-mail or a cell phone's text-messaging facility. Thus, the message board can display short messages, either to specific family members or to everyone. These messages can be posted either by handwriting, using a stylus on the display screen, sending an e-mail, or text-messaging from a mobile telephone (e.g., "Stuck in meeting—start dinner without me"). Figure 5.2B shows the message pad in action. One of the family's children, Will, has sent a text message asking to be picked up. He sent it to the central message board rather than to any particular person because he didn't know who might be available. Tim responded, adding a handwritten note so that other family members will know that the situation is being taken care of. This system accomplishes its goal of making people smarter by providing them with the tools they need but still letting them decide if, when, and how to make use of this assistance.

Other experimental smart homes have showcased a variety of related approaches. Imagine that you are in the middle of preparing to bake a cake when the telephone rings. You answer the phone, but when you return, how do you know where you left off? You recall adding flour to the bowl but aren't sure how many scoops. In the Georgia Institute of Technology's Aware Home, the "Cooks Collage" acts as a reminder. A television camera at the bottom of a cupboard photographs the cooking actions, displaying the steps taken. If you are interrupted in the middle of cooking, the display shows images of the last actions performed so you can readily remind yourself where you were. The philosophy here is very similar to that behind Microsoft's

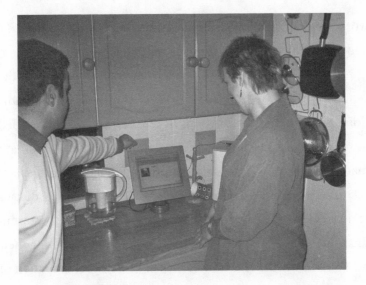

FIGURE 5.2

Microsoft Research kitchen display. A: The display can be put anywhere, here shown in the kitchen. B: One of the children (Will) has sent
a text message from his mobile phone to the message center asking to
be picked up (but not saying where he is). Another family member, Tim,
has responded, using a stylus to write a note on the display so the rest
of the family knows what is happening.

*(Photographs courtesy of the Socio-Digital Systems Group,
Microsoft Research Cambridge)*

work: augmentative technology should be voluntary, friendly, and cooperative. Use it or ignore it, as you wish.

Notice the important distinction between the devices of the Cambridge and Georgia Tech projects and those of the traditional smart home. Both groups of researchers could have tried to make the devices intelligent. In Cambridge, they could have made them sense who was in the room and change the displays accordingly, or they could have tried to read people's diaries and calendars, deciding for themselves what events to remind them of, what time they should be leaving the home for their next appointment. This is, indeed, a common preoccupation of researchers in the smart home field. Similarly, the researchers in Atlanta could have made an artificially intelligent assistant that read recipes, prompting and instructing every step of the way, or perhaps even an automated device that would make the cake itself. Instead, both groups devised systems that would fit smoothly into people's life styles. Both systems rely upon powerful, advanced technology, but the guiding philosophy for each group is augmentation, not automation.

Intelligent Things: Autonomous or Augmentative?

The examples of smart homes show two different directions in which research on smart things can move. One is toward intelligent autonomy, systems that attempt to infer the intentions of people. The other is toward intelligent augmentation, providing useful tools but letting people decide when and where they are to be used. Both systems have their merits, and both have their problems.

Augmentative tools are comforting, for they leave the decisions about activities to people. Thus, we can take them or leave them, choosing those that we feel aid our lives, ignoring those that do not. Moreover, because these are voluntary, different people can make different choices, so that people can choose whatever mix of technology suits their life style.

Autonomous devices can be useful when jobs are dull, dangerous, or dirty. Autonomous tools are useful when the task otherwise could not be accomplished. Consider search-and-rescue missions in dangerous situations, for example, into the rubble of buildings after major earthquakes, fires, or explosions. Moreover, in situations where people could do the task, it is often very nice when someone else does the work for us, even when that someone else is a machine.

Still, some tasks are simply not yet ready to be automated. "Automation always looks good on paper. . . . Sometimes you need real people," read the headline of a *New York Times* article commenting on the Denver, Colorado, airport's failed attempt to get its automated baggage-handling system to work properly. This system, the article claimed, "immediately became famous for its ability to mangle or misplace a good portion of everything that wandered into its path." After ten years of trying and the expenditure of hundreds of millions of dollars, the airport gave up and dismantled the system.

The Denver airport serves as an example of an automation attempt that seemed straightforward on paper but was made before the technology was up to the task. People's baggage comes in a wide assortment of shapes. It is placed arbitrarily on the luggage system's conveyer belts, then must be shuffled to many different connecting flights or baggage-delivery systems. The destination is marked by bar codes on the luggage tags, but those tags are bent, folded, and mutilated and are often hidden beneath handles, straps, or other luggage. This task has far too many irregularities and unknowns to be handled by today's systems.

Note that the airport shuttle trains that convey passengers between terminals at this same airport are completely automated and work smoothly and efficiently. The difference lies in the environment and the task, not the intelligence of the machines. With luggage, every piece is unique. With an airport shuttle, the route is completely fixed and predetermined. The train runs on tracks, so no steering is required. It can only move along the track, so the system only has to determine when it should move and how quickly. Simple sensors suffice to determine if anyone is standing in a doorway. When conditions are stable and the task well understood, when no mechanical agility is required and the unexpected happens infrequently, then automation can indeed take over. In these cases, automation works smoothly and efficiently and benefits everyone.

Shoshana Zuboff, a social psychologist at the Harvard Business School, has analyzed the impact of automation on a factory floor. The automatic equipment completely changed the social structure of the workers. On the one hand, it removed the operators from directly experiencing the production process. Whereas before they had felt the machines, smelled the fumes, and heard the sounds so that they could tell through their perceptions just how the procedure was going, now they were located in air-conditioned, sound-deadened control rooms, trying to imagine the state of affairs through dials, meters, and other indicators provided by the instrumentation. Although this change did speed up the process and increase uniformity, it also isolated the workers from the work and prevented the factory from making use of their years of experience with anticipating and correcting problems.

On the other hand, the use of computerized control equipment empowered the workers. Before, they were only given limited knowledge of the plant's operation and how their activities affected the performance of the company. Now, the computers helped keep them informed about the entire state of the plant, allowing them to understand the larger context to which their activities contributed. As a result, they could interact with middle and higher management on their own terms, by combining their knowledge of shop-floor operations with the information gleaned from their automation. Zuboff coined the term *informate* to describe the impact of the increased access to information afforded by automation to the workers: the workers were informated.

The Future of Design: Smart Things That Augment

People have many unique capabilities that cannot be replicated in machines, as least not yet. As we introduce automation and intelligence into the machines we use today, we need to be humble and recognize the problems and the potential for failure. We also need to recognize the vast discrepancy between the workings of people and of machines. On the whole, these responsive systems are valuable and helpful. But they can fail when they come across the fundamental limitations of human-machine interaction, most especially the lack of common ground that was discussed so extensively in chapter 2.

Autonomous, intelligent devices have proven invaluable in situations that are too dangerous for people; occasional failures are still far better than the risk of human life. Similarly, many intelligent devices have taken over the dull, routine tasks of maintaining our infrastructure, continually adjusting operating parameters and checking conditions in situations that are simply too tedious for people.

Augmentative technology has proven its worth. The recommender systems of many internet shopping sites are providing us with sensible suggestions, but because they are optional, they do not disrupt. Their occasional successes suffice to keep us content with their operation. Similarly, the augmentative technologies now being tested in smart homes, some described in this chapter, provide useful aids to everyday problems. Once again, their voluntary, augmentative status makes them palatable.

The future of design clearly lies in the development of smart devices that drive cars for us, make our meals, monitor our health, clean our floors, and tell us what to eat and when to exercise. Despite the vast differences between people and machines, if the task can be well specified, if the environmental conditions are reasonably well controlled, and if the machines and people can limit their interactions to the bare minimum, then intelligent, autonomous systems are valuable. The challenge is to add intelligent devices to our lives in a way that supports our activities, complements our skills, and adds to our pleasure, convenience, and accomplishments, but not to our stress.

CHAPTER SIX

Communicating with Our Machines

The whistling of the kettle and the sizzling of food cooking on the stove are reminders of an older era when everything was visible, everything made sounds, which allowed us to create mental models, conceptual models, of their operations. These models provided us with clues to help us troubleshoot when things did not go as planned, to know what to expect next, and to allow us to experiment.

Mechanical devices tend to be self-explaining. Their moving parts are visible and can be watched or manipulated. They make natural sounds that help us understand what is happening, so that even when we are not watching the machinery, we can often infer their state just from these sounds. Today, however, many of these powerful indicators are hidden from sight and sound, taken over by silent, invisible electronics. As a result, many devices operate silently, efficiently, and aside from the occasional clicking of a hard drive or the noise of a fan, they do not reveal much of their internal operations. We are left to the mercy of the designers for any information about the device's internal workings, what is happening within the device.

Communication, explanation, and understanding: these are the keys to working with intelligent agents, whether they are other people, animals, or machines. Teamwork requires coordination and communication, plus a good sense of what to expect, a good understanding of why things are, or are not, happening. This is true whether the team is composed of people, a skilled rider and horse, a driver and automobile, or a person and automated equipment. With animate beings, the communication is part of our biological heritage. We signal our emotional state through body language, posture, and facial expressions. We use language. Animals use body language and posture, as well as facial expressions. We can read the state of our pets through they way the hold their bodies, their tails, and their ears. A skilled rider can feel the horse's state of tension or relaxation.

Machines, though, are artificially created by people who often assume perfect performance on its part and, moreover, fail to understand the critical importance of a continuing dialogue between cooperating entities. If the machine is working perfectly, they tend to believe, why does anyone have to know what is happening? Why? Let me tell you a story.

I am seated in the fancy auditorium of IBM's Almaden Research Laboratories, situated in the beautiful, rolling hills just south of San Jose, California. The speaker at this conference, a professor of computer science at MIT—let me call him "Prof. M"—is extolling the virtues of his new program. After describing his work, Prof. M proudly starts to demonstrate it. First, he brings up a web page on the screen. Then, he does some magic with his mouse and keyboard, and after a few clicks and a little typing here and there, a new button appears on the page. "Ordinary people," explains the professor, "can add new controls to their web pages." (He never explains why anyone would want to.) "Now, watch as I show you that it works," he proudly announces. He clicks and we watch. And wait. And watch. Nothing happens.

Prof. M is puzzled. Should he restart the program? Restart the computer? The audience, filled with Silicon Valley's finest technocrats, shouts advice. IBM research scientists scurry back and forth, peering at his computer, getting down on hands and knees to follow the wiring. The seconds stretch into minutes. The audience starts to giggle.

Prof. M was so enamored of his technology that he never considered what would happen if it failed. It hadn't occurred to him to provide feedback for reassurance that things were working—or in this case, to provide clues when things didn't work. Later on, we discovered that the program was actually working perfectly, but there was no way of knowing this. The problem was that the security controls on IBM's internal network were not letting him gain access to the internet. Without feedback, however, without reassurance about the state of the program, nobody could tell just where the problem lay. The program lacked simple feedback to indicate that the click on the button had been detected, that the program was carrying out several steps of its internal instructions, that it had initiated an internet search, and that it was still waiting for the results to come back from that search.

Without feedback it wasn't possible to create the appropriate conceptual model. Any one of a dozen things could have failed: without evidence, there was no way to know. Prof. M had violated a fundamental design rule: provide continual awareness, without annoyance.

Feedback

"I'm at a meeting in Viña del Mar, Chile," starts an email from a colleague, "at a nice new Sheraton Hotel perched on the seawall. A lot of design effort went into it, including the elevators. A bank of them with up-down buttons at either end. The doors are glass and slide silently open and closed, with no sound to signal arrival or departure. With the typical ambient noise, you can't hear them, and unless standing close to an arriving elevator, can hardly see it move and can't tell when one is open. The only sign that an elevator is present is that the up-down signal light goes out—but you can't see that from the center of the elevator bank either. In my first day here, I missed elevators that came and went three times."

Feedback provides informative clues about what is happening, clues about what we should do. Without it, many simple operations fail, even one as simple as getting into an elevator. Proper feedback can make the difference between a pleasurable, successful system and one that frustrates and confuses. If the inappropriate use of feedback is frustrating with simple devices such as elevators, what will it be like with the completely automatic, autonomous devices of our future?

When we interact with people, we often form mental models of their internal thoughts, beliefs, and emotional states. We like to believe we know what they are thinking. Recall how frustrating it can be to interact with people who do not show any facial expressions, give no verbal responses? Are they even listening? Do they understand? Agree? Disagree? The interaction is strained and unpleasant. Without feedback, we can't operate, whether it is with an elevator, a person, or a smart machine.

Actually, feedback is probably even more essential when we interact with our machines than with other people. We need to know what is happening, what the machine has detected, what its state is, what actions it is about to do. Even when everything is working smoothly, we need reassurance that this is the case.

This applies to everyday things such as home appliances. How do we know they are working well? Fortunately, many appliances make noises: the hum of the refrigerator, the sounds of the dishwasher, clothes washer and drier, and the whir of the fan for home heating and cooling systems all provide useful, reassuring knowledge that the systems are on and are operating. The home computer has fans, and the hard drive makes clicking noises when active, once again, providing some reassurance. Notice that all these sounds are natural: they were not added artificially into the system by a designer or engineer but are natural side-effects of the working of physical devices. This very naturalness is what makes them so effective: differences in operation are often reflected in subtle differences in the sounds, so not only is it possible to tell if something is operating, but usually one can tell what operation is being done and whether or not the sounds are normal or possibly signify problems.

Newer systems have tried to reduce noise for good reason: the background level of noise in our homes and offices is disturbing. Yet, when systems make no sounds at all, it isn't possible to know if they are working. Just like the elevators of the opening quotation, sound can be informative. Quiet is good; silence may not be.

If sound is intrusive and annoying, even as a feedback mechanism, why not use lights? One problem is that a light, all by itself, is just as meaningless as the beeps that seem to erupt continually from my appliances. This is because the sounds are naturally created by the internal operation of the systems, whereas added on lights and beeps are artificial, signifying whatever arbitrary information the designer thought appropriate. Added-on lights almost always signify only some simple binary state: working or not, trouble or not, plugged in or not. There is no way for a person to know their meaning without recourse to a manual. There is no richness of interpretation, no subtlety: the light or beeps means that maybe things are good, or maybe bad, and all too often the person has to guess which.

Every piece of equipment has its own code for beeps, its own code for lights. A small red light visible on an appliance could mean that electric power is being applied, even though the appliance is off. Or it could mean that the unit is turned on, that it is working properly. Then again, red could signal that it is having trouble, and green could mean it is working properly. Some lights blink and flash; some change color. Different devices can use the same signals to indicate quite different things. Feedback is meaningless if it does not precisely convey a message.

When things go wrong, or when we wish to change the usual operation for a special occasion, we need feedback to instruct us how to do it. Then, we need feedback for reassurance that our request is being performed as we wished, and some indication about what will happen next: does the system revert to its normal mode, or is it now forever in the special mode? So, feedback is important for the following reasons:

- reassurance
- progress reports and time estimates
- learning
- special circumstances
- confirmation
- governing expectations

Today, many automatic devices do provide minimal feedback, but much of the time it is through bleeps and burps, ring tones and flashing lights. This feedback is more annoying than informing, and even when it does inform, it provides partial information at best. In commercial settings, such as manufacturing plants, electric generating plants, hospital operating rooms, or inside the cockpits of aircraft, when problems arise, many different monitoring systems and pieces of equipment sound alarms. The resulting cacophony can be so disturbing that the people involved may waste precious time turning all the alarms off so that they can concentrate on fixing the problems.

As we move toward an increasing number of intelligent, autonomous devices in our environment, we also need to transition toward a more supportive form of two-way interaction. People need information that facilitates discovery of the situation and that guides them in deciding how to respond or, for that matter, reassures them that no action is required. The interaction has to be continuous, yet nonintrusive, demanding little or no attention in most cases, requiring attention only when it is truly appropriate. Much of the time, especially when everything is working as planned, people only need to be kept in the loop, continually aware of the current state and of any possible problems ahead. Beeps won't work. Neither will spoken language. It has to be effective, yet in the periphery, so that it won't disturb other activities.

Who Deserves the Blame? The Technology or Ourselves?

In *The Design of Everyday Things*, I show that when people have difficulties with technology, invariably the technology or the design is at fault. "Don't blame yourself," I explain to my readers. "Blame the technology." Usually this is correct, but not always. Sometimes it is better when people blame themselves for a failure. Why? Because if it is the fault of the design or the technology, one can do nothing except become frustrated and complain. If it is a person's fault, perhaps the person can change and learn to work the technology. Where might this be true? Let me tell you about the Apple Newton.

In 1993, I left the comfortable life of academia and joined Apple Computer. My baptism into the world of commerce was rapid and rough—from being on the study team to determine whether and how AT&T should purchase Apple Computer, or at the very least form a joint venture, to watching over the launch of the Apple Newton. Both ventures failed, but the Newton failure was the more instructive case.

Ah, the Newton. A brilliant idea, introduced with great hoopla and panache. The Newton was the first sensible personal data assistant. It was a small device by the standards of the time, portable, and controlled solely by handwriting on a touch-sensitive screen. The story of the Newton is complex—books have been written about it—but here let me talk about one of its most deadly sins: the Newton's handwriting recognition system.

The Newton claimed to be able to interpret handwriting, transforming it into printed text. Great, except that this was back in 1993, and up to that time, there were no successful handwriting recognition systems. Handwriting recognition poses a very difficult technical challenge, and even today there are no completely successful systems. The Newton system was developed by a group of Russian scientists and programmers in a small company, Paragraph International. The system was technically sophisticated, but it flunked my rule of human-machine interaction, which is to be intelligible.

The system first performed a mathematical transformation on the handwriting strokes of each word into a location within an abstract, mathematical space of many dimensions, then matched what the user had written to its database of English words, picking the word that was closest in distance within this abstract space. If this sentence confuses you about how Newton recognized words, then you understand properly. Even sophisticated users of Newton could not explain the kinds of errors that it made. When the word recognition system worked, it was very, very good, and when it failed, it was horrid. The problem was caused by the great difference between the sophisticated mathematical multidimensional space that it was using and a person's perceptual judgments. There seemed to be no actual relationship between what was written and what the system produced. In fact, there was a relationship, but it was in the realm of sophisticated mathematics, invisible to the person who was trying to make sense of its operation.

The Newton was released with great fanfare. People lined up for hours to be among the first to get one. Its ability to recognize handwriting was touted as a great innovation. In fact, it failed miserably, providing rich fodder for cartoonist Garry Trudeau, an early adopter. He used his comic strip, *Doonesbury*, to poke fun at the Newton. Figure 6.1 shows the best-known example, a strip that detractors and fans of the Newton labeled "Egg Freckles." I don't know if writing the words "Catching on?" would really turn into "Egg freckles?" but given the bizarre output that the Newton often produced, it's entirely possible.

FIGURE 6.1

Garry Trudeau's *Doonesbury* strip "Egg Freckles," widely credited with dooming the success of Apple Computer's Newton. The ridicule was deserved, but the public forum of this popular comic strip was devastating. The real cause? Completely unintelligible feedback. Doonesbury © 1993 G. B. Trudeau.

The point of this discussion is not to ridicule the Newton but rather to learn from its shortcomings. The lesson is about human-machine communication: always make sure a system's response is understandable and interpretable. If it isn't what the person expected, there should be an obvious action the person can take to get to the desired response.

Several years after "Egg Freckles," Larry Yeager, working in Apple's Advanced Technology Group, developed a far superior method for recognizing handwriting. Much more importantly, however, the new system, called "Rosetta," overcame the deadly flaw of the Paragraph system: errors could now be understood. Write "hand" and the system might recognize "nand": people found this acceptable because the system got most of the letters right, and the one it missed, "h," does look like an "n." If you write "Catching on?" and get "Egg freckles?" you blame the Newton, deriding it as "a stupid machine." But if you write "hand" and get "nand," you blame yourself: "Oh, I see," you might say to yourself, "I didn't make the first line on the 'h' high enough so it thought it was an 'n'."

Notice how the conceptual model completely reverses the notion of where blame is to be placed. Conventional wisdom among human-centered designers is that if a device fails to deliver the expected results, it is the device or its design that should be blamed. When the machine fails to recognize handwriting, especially when the reason for the failure is obscure, people blame the machine and become frustrated and angry. With Rosetta, however, the situation is completely reversed: people are quite happy to place the blame on themselves if it appears that they did something wrong, especially when what they are required to do appears reasonable. Rather than becoming frustrated, they simply resolve to be more careful next time.

This is what really killed the Newton: people blamed it for its failure to recognize their handwriting. By the time Apple released a sensible, successful handwriting recognizer, it was too late. It was not possible to overcome the earlier negative reaction and scorn. Had the Newton featured a less accurate, but more understandable, recognition system from the beginning, it might have succeeded. The early Newton is a good example of how any design unable to give meaningful feedback is doomed to failure in the marketplace.

When Palm released their personal digital assistant (initially called the "Palm Pilot") in 1996, they used an artificial language, "Graffiti," that required the user to learn a new way of writing. Graffiti used artificial letter shapes, similar to the normal printed alphabet, but structured so as to make the machine's task as easy as possible. The letters were similar enough to everyday printing that they could be learned without much effort. Graffiti didn't try to recognize whole words, it operated letter by letter, and so, when it made an error, it was only on a single letter, not the entire word. In addition, it was easy to find a reason for the error in recognition. These understandable, sensible errors made it easy for people to see what they might have done wrong and provided hints as to how to avoid the mistake the next time. The errors were actually reassuring, helping everyone develop a good mental model for how the recognition worked, helping people gain confidence, and helping them improve their handwriting. Newton failed; Palm succeeded.

Feedback is essential to the successful understanding of any system, essential for our ability to work in harmony with machines. Today, we rely too much on alarms and alerts that are too sudden, intrusive, and not very informative. Signals that simply beep, vibrate, or flash usually don't indicate what is wrong, only that something isn't right. By the time we have figured out the problem, the opportunity to take corrective action may have passed. We need a more continuous, more natural way of staying informed of the events around us. Recall poor Prof. M: without feedback, he couldn't even figure out if his own system was working.

What are some ways to provide better methods of feedback? The foundation for the answer was laid in chapter 3, "Natural Interaction": implicit communication, natural sounds and events, calm, sensible signals, and the exploitation of natural mappings between display devices and our interpretations of the world.

Natural, Deliberate Signals

Watch someone helping a driver maneuver into a tight space. The helper may stand beside the car, visible to the driver, holding two hands apart to indicate the distance remaining between the car and the obstacle. As the car moves, the hands move closer together. The nice thing about this method of guidance is that it is natural: it does not have to be agreed upon beforehand; no instruction or explanation is needed.

Implicit signals can be intentional, either deliberately created by a person, as in the example above, or deliberately created in a machine by the designer. There are natural ways to communicate with people that convey precise information without words and with little or no training. Why not use these methods as a way of communicating between people and machines?

Many modern automobiles have parking assistance devices that indicate how close the auto is to the car ahead or behind. An indicator emits a series of beeps: beep (pause), beep (pause), beep. As the car gets closer to the obstacle, the pauses get shorter, so the rate of beeping increases. When the beeps become continuous, it is time to stop: the car is about to hit the obstacle. As with the hand directions, this natural signal can be understood by a driver without instruction.

Natural signals, such as the clicks of the hard drive after a command or the familiar sound of water boiling in the kitchen, keep people informed about what is happening in the environment. These signals offer just enough information to provide feedback, but not enough to add to cognitive workload. Mark Weiser and John Seely Brown, two research scientists working at what was then the Xerox Corporation's Palo Alto Research Center, called this "calm technology," which "engages both the center and the periphery of our attention, and in fact moves back and forth between the two." The center is what we are attending to, the focal point of conscious attention. The periphery includes all that happens outside of central awareness, while still being noticeable and effective. In the words of Weiser and Brown:

> We use "periphery" to name what we are attuned to without attending to explicitly. Ordinarily when driving our attention is centered on the road, the radio, our passenger, but not the noise of the engine. But an unusual noise is noticed immediately, showing that we were attuned to the noise in the periphery, and could come quickly to attend to it. . . . A calm technology will move easily from the periphery of our attention, to the center, and back. This is fundamentally encalming, for two reasons.

First, by placing things in the periphery, we are able to attune to many more things than we could if everything had to be at the center. Things in the periphery are attuned to by the large portion of our brains devoted to peripheral (sensory) processing. Thus, the periphery is informing without overburdening.

Second, by recentering something formerly in the periphery, we take control of it.

Note the phrase "informing without overburdening." That is the secret of calm, natural communication.

Natural Mappings

In *The Design of Everyday Things*, I explain how what I call "natural mappings" can be used to lay out the controls for appliances. For example, stoves traditionally have four burners, arranged in a two-dimensional rectangle. Yet, the controls invariably are laid out in a one-dimensional line. As a result, people frequently turn on or off the wrong burner, even if the controls are labeled, in part because there is no natural relationship between controls and burners, in part because each stove model seems to use a different rule to map controls to burners. Human factors professionals have long demonstrated that if the controls were laid out in a rectangular array, no labels would be needed: each control would match the corresponding spatial position of the appropriate burner. Some stove manufacturers do this well. Others do it badly. And some do it well for one model, but badly for another.

The scientific principles for proper mapping are clear. In the case of the spatial arrangement of controls, lights, and burners, I define *natural mapping* to mean that controls should be laid out in a manner spatially analogous to the layout of the devices they control and, as much as possible, on the same plane. But why restrict natural mappings to spatial relationships? The principle can be extended to numerous other domains.

Sound has been discussed at length because it is such an important source of feedback. Sound clearly plays a valuable role in keeping us naturally informed about the state of things. Vibration plays an equally important role. In the early days of aviation, when an airplane was about to stall, the lack of lift would cause the control stick to vibrate. Today, with larger airplanes and automatic control systems, pilots no longer can feel these natural warning signals, but they have been reintroduced artificially. When the airplane computes that it is approaching a stall, the system warns by shaking the control stick. "Stick Shaker," this function is called, and it provides a valuable warning of stall conditions.

When power steering was first introduced into automobiles, augmenting the driver's efforts with hydraulic or electric power, drivers had difficulty controlling the vehicle: without feedback from the road, driving skills are badly diminished. So, modern vehicles carefully control how much effort is required and reintroduced some of the road vibrations. "Road feel" provides essential feedback.

Rumble strips on highways warn drivers when they are drifting off the road. When they were first introduced, the only tool available to the engineers was the road itself, so they cut slots into the roadway, causing a "rumble" when the car's wheels went over them. This same principle is used as a speed warning: a series of slots is placed perpendicular to the road where the driver should slow down or stop. The strips get closer and closer together, so if the driver fails to slow sufficiently, resulting rumble increases in frequency. Even though these rumble strip cues are artificially induced, they have proven effective.

Some researchers have experimented successfully with vibrators in the automobile seat, vibrating the right part of the seat when the car is drifting to the right, the left when the car drifts left, mimicking the effect of rumble strips. Similarly, the front of the car or of the seat can vibrate when the car gets too close to the car ahead or exceeds safe speed limits. These signals are effective in informing the driver of the location of the vehicle relative to the road and other cars. They illustrate two different principles: natural mapping and continual awareness (without annoyance). The seat vibrations provide a natural mapping between the position at which the vibration is felt and the position of the nearby vehicles. Because the seat continually vibrates (gently) to the presence of surrounding vehicles, the information is continually available. Yet, the vibrations are subtle, nonintrusive, just like the sounds surrounding us—always letting us know what is happening, but never demanding full attention, therefore never intruding upon consciousness. This is continual information without annoyance.

Natural signals provide effective communication. The lessons of these chapters can be summarized in six succinct rules, all of which focus on the nature of the communication between people and machines. When people interact with one another, they follow a wide range of conventions and protocols, often subconsciously. The rules of interaction have evolved over tens of thousands of years as a fundamental natural component of human social interaction and culture. We don't have the luxury of waiting thousands of years for a similar richness of interaction between us and our machines, but fortunately, we do not need to wait. We already know many of the rules. Here they are, spelled out explicitly so that designers and engineers can implement them in the innards of machines:

- Design Rule One: Provide rich, complex, and natural signals.
- Design Rule Two: Be predictable.
- Design Rule Three: Provide a good conceptual model.
- Design Rule Four: Make the output understandable.
- Design Rule Five: Provide continual awareness, without annoyance.
- Design Rule Six: Exploit natural mappings to make interaction understandable and effective.

As more and more automation enters all aspects of our lives, the challenge for designers is to keep people engaged, to provide the correct amount of natural, environmental information so that people can take advantage of automation to free themselves to do other things, yet can take control when the conditions require it.

When it comes to intelligent systems, there are problems in maintaining this balance. Foremost is the lack of common ground between people and machines, a problem I believe is fundamental. This is not something that can be cured by new designs: it will take decades of research to understand these issues fully. Someday we may make intelligent agents that are much more animate, more complete. Then, we can start to add sophistication, establish common ground, and allow real conversation to take place. We are a long way away from developing machines that can do this.

For effective interaction with machines, the machines must be predictable and understandable. People must be able to understand their state, their actions, and what is about to happen. People need to be able to interact in a natural manner. And the awareness and understanding of the machines' states and activities should be generated in a way that is continuous, unobtrusive, and effective. That's the bottom line. This demanding set of requirements has not really been achieved by today's machines. It is the goal to strive for.

CHAPTER SEVEN

The Future of Everyday Things

"What if the everyday objects around us came to life? What if they could sense our presence, our focus of attention, and our actions, and could respond with relevant information, suggestions, and actions?" Would you like that? Professor Pattie Maes at MIT's Media Laboratory hopes you will. She is trying to develop just such devices. "For example," she says, "we are creating technologies that make it possible for the book you are holding to tell you what passages you may be particularly interested in . . . and the picture of your grandmother on the wall keeps you abreast of how she is doing when you glance up at it."

"Mirror, mirror on the wall, Who's the fairest of them all?" Snow White's cruel stepmother posed this question to a wondrous, magical mirror that always told the truth, no matter how much it might pain the listener. Today's technologists are contemplating mirrors that are more considerate and that answer easier questions:

Mirror, mirror, on the wall,

Does this clothing match at all?

The mirror of tomorrow will do things Snow White's mirror never even dreamed of: share your image with loved ones, sending it to cell phones and computers for them to critique. The modern magical mirror will do more than answer questions or show you off to others. It will change your image: make you look slimmer or drape new clothes over your image so you can see what they look like on you without the bother of trying them on. It will even be able to change your hairstyle.

Brown and blue are not for you.

Try this jacket. Use this shoe.

Smart technologies have the capacity to enhance pleasure, simplify lives, and add to our safety. If only they could really work flawlessly; if only we could learn how to use them.

Once upon a time, in a different century and a faraway place, I wrote about people who had trouble working their microwave ovens, setting the time on their appliances, turning on and off the correct burners on their stoves, and even opening and shutting doors. The faraway time was the 1980s; the faraway place was England. And the people were just plain ordinary people, children and adults, undereducated and overeducated. I started my book—originally titled *The Psychology of Everyday Things* and renamed *The Design of Everyday Things*—with a quotation about the distinguished founder and CEO of a major computer company, who confessed that he couldn't figure out how to heat a cup of coffee in his company's microwave oven.

We are now entering a new era in which everyday objects are growing smarter and smarter. This is happening in many domains, but nowhere as quickly as in the realm of the automobile. And what is in the automobile today will be in the kitchen, bathroom, and living room tomorrow. Intelligent Vehicles is a development program by the world's automobile manufacturers to automate many of the components of driving, adding to people's comfort and safety. Cars that drive themselves are not far away: cars that partially drive themselves are here today.

"Intelligent agents," "smart homes," "ambient environments": these are the names of multiple research projects in universities and research laboratories today. They include systems that select your music, control the room lighting—both brightness and color—and generally modify the environment, in part to add pleasure and comfort, in part to be more sensitive to environmental issues, such as energy usage. Other programs monitor the food you eat, the activities you perform, and even the people you interact with.

In market-driven economies, new services are continually being offered to the public, not because there is demand but because the companies need to increase their sales. I've talked with the designers and service providers of mobile telephones and to the designers of home appliances. "Everyone already owns a mobile phone in this country," I was told in South Korea, "so we have to think of additional services to offer: phones that tell you when you are near your friends, that you can use to pay bills, that identify who you are, and that provide transportation schedules." Phones that sense your moods and make suggestions.

Automobile makers long ago realized that cars could be thought of as fashion objects, going out of style on a regular basis, encouraging people to keep up to date. Phone makers have done the same thing. This is so true of watches that they are sold as jewelry, not technology. Refrigerators now have colorful displays on their front panels (right next to the ice and water dispensers) that tell you whatever the designer thinks you want to know. In the future, foods will have computer-readable tags so that the refrigerator will know what is inside it and what you are putting in or taking out. It will know the expiration dates of the items, as well as your weight and diet. It will continually make suggestions.

Machines will become more social, talking with their owners, but also talking with one another. One movie rental company already compares the movies you watch and the ratings you give them with those of people you have listed as friends, recommending movies they liked which you haven't yet seen, e-mailing you their findings. Perhaps your refrigerator will compare its contents with that of your neighbors' refrigerators and recommend foods. Entertainment systems will compare music and video preferences, and your television set will compare the shows you watch with those watched by your neighbors. "Your friends are watching *12 Monkeys* right now," it might say. "I've turned it on for you as well, but even though they've already started, I'll start yours from the beginning."

At the same time that our machines are getting more intelligent, with more and more capabilities and communication facilities, there has been a revolution in materials. Need a lightweight, extremely strong material that can be embedded in the human body without deterioration and without harm to the body? Sure, coming up. Need environmentally friendly materials that are easily recyclable or biologically degradable? Sure, coming up. Need flexibility? Need a cloth that can display pictures? Sure, coming up. New methods of displaying and interacting with art, music, images, and sounds proliferate. Sensors allow detection of movement and identification of people and objects. New displays allow messages and images to be projected seemingly anywhere. Some materials are tiny, microscopic (nanotechnology). Some are large (bridges and ships). Some are biological, some metallic, some ceramic, some plastic, and some organic. Materials are changing.

These materials can be used to fabricate new items in the home itself. Today's fax machines and printers are capable of reproducing words and pictures two-dimensionally on paper. In the very near future, we will see faxes and printers that produce three-dimensional copies. Did your child make a nice clay sculpture you want to show the grandparents? Put it in the 3-D fax, and it will be recreated at their home. Did the hinge on a kitchen appliance break? Have a new one faxed to you. Or design your own objects, drawing them on the home screen and creating them as real, physical devices.

The 3-D fax works by scanning the object, using a laser beam, multiple photographs, or both, creating an accurate digital representation that depicts the object's precise shape. Then, this representation is sent to the receiving station, which recreates the object with a 3-D printer. These printers now work by a wide variety of means, but most construct the object layer by layer. A very thin layer of material—often a plastic or polymer, sometimes a powdered metal—is deposited to create an exact re-creation of the cross-sectional shape of the object at one level. That layer is then hardened, using a hardening agent such as heat or ultra violet light, and the process repeats itself for the next layer.

Today, 3-D printing technology is only in companies and universities, but the prices are now getting low enough and the quality good enough that it is easy to contemplate every home having a 3-D printer in the future. Note that the 3-D printing technology doesn't require that there be an original object to copy: any drawing will do, as long as it specifies the piece precisely. It won't be long before anyone can use a home sketching kit to produce the proper drawing, and shortly thereafter the home printer will have created the actual physical object. If you can draw it, you can make it. "You didn't have enough dinner plates for your guests," your house might announce, "so I took the liberty of printing more. I made sure to use the same pattern."

What about Robots?

Robots are coming, but what does this mean? Many experts would have you believe that robots are already here, capable of a wide variety of activities, including managing health care—for instance, monitoring medication compliance—handling security, performing education services, running errands, and providing entertainment. Robots are, of course, used in manufacturing, in search-and-rescue missions, and in the military. When we discuss reasonably priced machines for personal use, however, most of these so-called applications are more dream than reality, with unreliable mechanisms barely able to get through demonstrations.

FIGURE 7.1

The home robot of the future? This is what we dream of, but much as I might like to be served by a robot, as shown in the drawing by Alison Wong, this development is unlikely to come to pass anytime soon. See the text for the reasons.

Given that any successful product for the home must be affordable, reliable, safe, and usable by everyday people, what might a home robot do? Would it look like a human servant (Figure 7.1)? In the home, form will probably follow function. A kitchen robot might be built into the counter space, with dishwasher, pantry, coffee maker, and cooking units arranged so that they can communicate with one another and pass items readily back and forth. An entertainment robot might take on a humanoid appearance. And robots that vacuum or mow lawns will look like, well, vacuum cleaners and lawn mowers.

Making robots work well is incredibly difficult. Their sensory apparatus is limited because sensors are expensive and interpretation (especially commonsense knowledge) is still more suited to research than deployment. Robotic arms are expensive to build and not very reliable. This limits the range of possibilities: Mowing and vacuuming? Sure. Sorting laundry? Hard, but doable. Picking up dirty items around the home? Doubtful. How about assistance for the elderly or those who need medical supervision? This is a booming area of exploration, but I am skeptical. Today's devices are not reliable, versatile, or intelligent enough—not yet, anyway. Many so-called robots are in actuality remotely controlled by people. Autonomous robots that interact with people are difficult to design. Moreover, the social aspects of the interaction, including the need for common ground, are far more complex than the technical ones, something technology-driven enthusiasts typically fail to recognize.

Three likely directions for the future are entertainment, home appliances, and education. We can start with today's existing devices and slowly add on intelligence, manipulative ability, and function. The market for robots that entertain by being cute and cuddly is already well established. Robot vacuum cleaners and lawn mowers already exist. The definition of "robot" varies widely, often being used to refer to anything that is mobile, even though it is controlled by a human. I prefer to restrict the term to autonomous systems. I would classify intelligent home appliances as robots: many coffee makers, microwave ovens, dishwashers, and clothes washers and dryers have more intelligence and actuators than robot vacuum cleaners—and they are also a lot more expensive. But they don't move around the room, which for many people disqualifies them from the label "robot."

Education is a powerful possibility. A solid base of devices already aid learning. Today's robots can read aloud in engaging voices. They can be cute and lovable—witness the responses to the multiple quasi-intelligent animals on the toy market. A robot could very well interact with a child, offering educational benefits as well. Why not have the robot help the child learn the alphabet or teach reading, vocabulary, pronunciation, basic arithmetic, and maybe basic reasoning? Why not music and art, geography, and history? And why restrict this technology to children? Adults, too, can benefit from robot-assisted learning.

Now, this is a direction deserving exploration: robot as teacher—not to replace school or human contact and interaction, but to supplement them. The beauty here is that these tasks are well within the abilities of today's devices. They don't require much mobility or sophisticated manipulators. Many technologists dream of implementing Neil Stephenson's children's tutor from his novel *The Diamond Age: Or, A Young Lady's Illustrated Primer*. Here is a worthy challenge.

All of the problems discussed in this book about autonomous assistants apply with even greater force to robots. So-called general-purpose robots—those of movie and science fiction fame—suffer from the common ground problem. How will we communicate with them? How will we synchronize our activities so neither of us gets in the other's way? How will we instruct them? My suspicion is that when they finally start to appear, they will barely communicate: they will take instructions (clean the house, pick up the dirty dishes, bring me a drink), and then they will go off to do these tasks, leaving us humans to learn their habits and keep out of their way.

Intelligent home appliances, robot vacuum cleaners and lawn mowers are really special-purpose robots. They do not have a communication problem because they have a limited repertoire of activities, so they offer only a few alternatives to their owners. As a result, we know what to expect of them and how to interact. For these devices, the common ground required for interaction consists of our mutual understanding of the tasks they are designed to perform, the strengths and limitations of their abilities, and the environment they work in. The result is fewer miscommunications, fewer difficulties than with more general-purpose devices.

Robots have been of value to explorers of dangerous or difficult-to-reach locations, such as the insides of volcanoes, sewer pipes, or the surface of Mars or the moon. They are well suited for assessing damage and locating survivors after accidents, earthquakes, or terrorist attacks. Yet, these are hardly everyday activities, and for these applications, cost is not critical. Still, these special applications are giving us the experience necessary to get the costs down and make these devices available for everyone.

Finally, there is one other type of robot to come: interconnected, communicating robots. Cars are already starting to talk to one another and to the highways so they can synchronize intersections and lane changing. In the near future, cars will let restaurants know their location so they can suggest menus to the passengers. Clothes washing machines are starting to talk to clothes driers so the drier knows just what to expect and what setting to use. In the United States, people have separate washing machines and driers, so if this pattern persists, someday, the clothes will be automatically transferred from washer to dryer. (In Europe and Asia, a single machine often does both, making the transition between the two activities much simpler.) In restaurants and homes, dishes will automatically be put into the dishwasher and then automatically sent to the pantry. Home appliances will synchronize their operations, the better to control noise and minimize energy costs by delaying their operations for off-peak hours.

Robots are arriving, and as they do, we will run into precisely the problems I've been discussing throughout this book. They are starting out as toys, entertainment devices, and simple pets. Then they will become companions, reading stories and tutoring topics such as reading, language instruction, spelling, and mathematics. They will allow us to monitor the home (and our elderly relatives) from a distance. And soon, the appliances in our homes and automobiles will become part of intelligent communication networks. Special-purpose robots will increase in number, in power, and in the range of tasks they are able to perform. General-purpose robots will arrive last of all, decades from now.

Technology Changes, but People Stay the Same—or Do They?

It used to be a truism among scholars that although technologies change, people stay the same. The biological species called *Homo sapiens* changes very slowly through the process of natural evolution. Moreover, even individuals change their behavior slowly, and this natural conservatism dampens the impact of technological change. Although science and technology make rapid changes, month-by-month, year-by-year, people's behaviors and cultures take decades to change. Biological change takes place over millennia.

But what if the changes in technology impact us as human beings, not just our physical artifacts? What if we implant bionic enhancers or do genetic modification? Today, we already implant artificial lenses for the eye, prosthetic auditory devices for the ears, and soon vision enhancements for those who cannot see. Some surgical operations can make eyes superior to normally functioning ones. Implants and biological enhancers, even for everyday life for otherwise normal people, no longer seem like the dreams of science fiction but are becoming both real and realistic. Athletes already modify their natural abilities through drugs and operations. Can brain enhancement be far behind?

But even without genetic design, biomagic, or surgery, the human brain does change as a result of experience. Thus, London taxi drivers, famous for their detailed knowledge of London streets, are known to increase the size of their brain structures in the hippocampus through the years of training they undergo to acquire that knowledge. It isn't just London taxi drivers, however. Many experts, it seems, have expanded brain structures in the areas responsible for their expertise. Experience does change the brain. The evidence suggests that extended contact with technology—long hours spent practicing musical instruments or typing with the thumbs on cell phones or other hand-held devices—constitutes the kind of practice that can affect the brain.

Are children growing up with different brains because of their exposure to technology? I've been asked that question for years, and for years I've said that the brain is determined by biology, and evolution is unaffected by our experiences. Well, I was right in saying that brain biology does not change: the brain at birth of people born today is very much the same as human brains have been for thousands of years. But I was also wrong. Experience does change the brain, especially prolonged, early experience of children.

Exercise makes muscles stronger; mental practice makes regions of the brain function better. Brain changes brought about by learning and practice are not inherited, just as increased muscle mass is not passed from one generation to the next. Still, as technology enters the life of children at an earlier and earlier age, it will impact how they respond, think, and behave. Their brains will be modified early in life to accommodate these new skills.

Many more changes are possible. Biological technology, perhaps coupled with implanted devices for perception, memory, and even strength enhancement, is slowly, inevitably coming. Future generations may not be content with natural biology. Battles will arise between those who are modified and those who resist. Science fiction will become science fact.

As we move forward, society needs to address the impact of all this change on individuals and societies. Designers are at the forefront of these concerns, for it is the designer who translates ideas into reality. Today, more than ever before, designers need to understand the social impact of their actions.

Conforming to Our Technology

Science Finds,

Industry Applies,

Man Conforms

— Motto of the 1933 Chicago World's Fair.

People Propose,

Science Studies,

Technology Conforms

— A person-centered motto for the twenty-first century.

In my book *Things That Make Us Smart*, I argue that it is technology that should conform to us, not, as the 1933 World's Fair motto would have it, we who should conform to technology. I wrote that book in 1993, and since then I have changed my mind. Sure, I would prefer that machines adapt to people. In the end, though, machines are simply too limited in capability. We humans are flexible and adaptable. They are rigid and unchanging. We are more capable of change. We either take technology as it is or go without.

The danger of stating that people must adapt to machines is that some designers and engineers will interpret the recommendation out of context, believing it gives them free rein to design however they wish, optimizing their work for machine efficiency and ease of design, engineering, and construction. But the statement is not an excuse for inappropriate design. We certainly shouldn't have to adapt to that.

We need the best designs possible, ones that are sensitive to people, that follow all the best rules of human-centered, activity-centered design, designs that follow the rules put forth within this book (summarized in chapter 6, page 152). Even in the best of cases, however, when the best designers have done the best jobs possible, the machines will still be limited. They will still be inflexible, rigid, and demanding. Their sensors will be limited, their capabilities different from ours. And then there is that huge gulf of common ground.

Who would have thought that we would have to explain ourselves to our machines? Well, we do. We have to explain to our automobile that we really want to turn left. The day will come when we have to tell the vacuum cleaner that we don't want it to clean the living room right now, thank you. We may have to inform our kitchens that, please, we are hungry now, and we would like to eat, and tell our music players that we are going out for a run, so would it pick music appropriate to our pace.

It helps if the machines know what we intend to do, just as it helps if we know what they intend. Once again, though, because machine intelligence is so limited, the burden lies with us. These adaptations will end up benefiting all of us, just as making a home or place of business accessible to those with handicaps turns out to be useful for everyone.

It's important to keep in mind that adapting to technology is hardly a new phenomenon. From the first tools onward, the introduction of each has changed the way we behave. In the 1800s, we paved roads for carts and vehicles. In the 1900s, we wired our homes when electricity replaced gas lines, added pipes once plumbing and toilets came indoors, and installed wires and outlets for telephones, television sets, then internet connections. In the 2000s, we will redo our homes for the benefit of our machines.

Coincidentally, in the 2000s many nations face an aging population. People will discover that they must restructure their homes and buildings to accommodate their elderly relatives—or themselves. They may have to add elevators, provide entrance ramps, replace knobs with levers on faucets and doors, and enlarge doorways to allow the passage of wheelchairs. Light switches and electrical outlets will be moved for easier access; the height of kitchen counters, sinks, and tables will have to be

FIGURE 7.2

"Transaction refused: You have enough shoes." This figure, by the Belgium advertising agency Duval Guillaume Antwerp, hints at the future of intelligent technology. Actually, the store's credit card terminal would want to encourage you to buy matching socks, belts, or shirts, but your personal assistant might very well try to stop you. So now, not only do we have intelligent systems offering advice, but we might have fights and conflicts.

(Photograph and permission to reproduce provided by the photographer, Kris Van Beek, www.krisvanbeek.com)

adjusted. Ironically, these are the very same changes that will make life easier for machines, even as we bring in those machines to make life easier for the elderly. Why? Because machines share with the elderly similar limitations in mobility, agility, and vision.

Will we reach the day of dueling intelligences: Your refrigerator enticing you to eat while your scale insists you shouldn't? The store enticing you to buy, but the personal assistant inside your mobile phone resisting? Even your television and cell phone might gang up on you. But we can fight back. The personal advisor of the future will look out for you, perhaps residing inside the very same television or telephone that is trying to sell you that other pair of shoes. "No," says one helpful machine (Figure 7.2), "transaction refused: you have enough shoes." "Yes," says another machine, "you need new shoes for the formal dinner next week."

The Science of Design

Design: The deliberate shaping of the environment in ways that satisfy individual and societal needs.

Design cuts across all disciplines, be it the arts or sciences, humanities or engineering, law or business. In universities, the practical is often judged less valuable than the abstract and theoretical. Universities, moreover, put each discipline into separate schools and departments, where people mainly talk to others within their own narrowly defined categories. This compartmentalization is optimal for developing specialists who understand their narrow area in great depth. It is not well suited for the development of generalists whose work cuts across disciplines. Even when the university tries to overcome this deficit by establishing new, multidisciplinary programs, the new program soon becomes its own discipline and grows more and more specialized each year.

Designers must be generalists who can innovate across disciplines. In turn, they must be able to call upon specialists to help develop their designs and to ensure that the components are appropriate and practical. This is a new kind of activity, different from what is normally taught in the academic departments of universities. It is somewhat akin to the way schools of management work. For example, they train managers who must also be generalists, able to understand the many divisions and functions of a company, able to call upon specialists within each area. Perhaps design belongs in the school of business.

Design, today, is taught and practiced as an art form or craft, not as a science with known principles that have been verified through experimentation and that can be used to derive new design approaches. Most design schools today teach through mentoring and apprenticeship. Students and beginning professionals practice their craft in workshops and studios under the watchful eyes of instructors and mentors. This is an excellent way to learn a craft, but not a science.

It is time for a science of design. After all, we know a lot about design from the many related disciplines: the social sciences and the arts, engineering, and business. To date, engineers have attempted to apply formal methods and algorithms that optimize the mechanical and mathematical aspects of a design but tend to ignore the social and the aesthetic. The artistic side, on the other hand, fiercely resists systematization, believing it will destroy the creative heart of design. However, as we move toward the design of intelligent machines, rigor is absolutely essential. It can't be the cold, objective rigor of the engineer, for this focuses only on what can be measured as opposed to what is important. We need a new approach, one that combines the precision and rigor of business and engineering, the understanding of social interactions, and the aesthetics of the arts.

What does the rise of the smart machine mean for designers? In the past, we had to think about how people would interact with technology. Today, we also need to take the machine's point of view. Smart machines are all about interaction, symbiosis, and cooperation, both with people and with other smart machines. This is a new discipline, with very little past work to guide us, despite the development of fields whose names sound as if they were ideally suited for our needs, fields such as interactive design, supervisory control, automation design, and human-machine interaction. There is enough known about human psychology to make a beginning. The applied fields of human factors and ergonomics have provided many useful studies and techniques. We need to build on these.

The future puts new demands on our designs. In the past, we merely used our products. In the future, we will be in more of a partnership with them as collaborators, bosses, and, in some cases, servants and assistants. More and more, we supervise and oversee, even as we ourselves are being supervised and overseen.

Smart autonomous machines are not the only direction of the future. We will inhabit virtual worlds, where we travel effortlessly through artificially created environments and converse with the displayed images of avatars, perhaps unable even to distinguish the real from the artificial. Entertainment will change drastically because of the social interaction of people across the world and because of the power of simulations to make us believe we are experiencing new events, new worlds.

Research laboratories are already studying three-dimensional spaces, such as the one shown in Figure 7.3, which provides detailed images of dynamic worlds, displayed on the floor, walls, and ceiling of the room. It is an amazing experience, conducive both to education and entertainment. Note, too, that it is a shared experience, as groups of people can explore the environment together. The figure fails to capture the power of the experience. This is a future that is emotionally appealing and engaging as well as educational and entertaining.

We are in for confusing times and exciting times, dangerous times and enjoyable times, for viscerally exciting interactions, behaviorally satisfying ones, and reflectively pleasurable ones. Or perhaps, we are not. How well these will succeed will depend on the design of future things.

FIGURE 7.3

The entertainment/learning system of the future. These photographs were taken at the Virtual Reality Applications Center at Iowa State University. I am standing inside a "cave," surrounded by extremely high-definition images in front, behind, on the sides, and on the floor and ceiling. In the top image, I am inside a plant cell, learning biology. In the bottom one, I'm on a beach. This is a multi-million-dollar installation, with one hundred million pixels of displays, and the computers required to drive the images take so much power that special circuits are required, with huge air conditioners to keep them cool. But what is in the laboratory today will be in the home in a decade or two.

(Photographs taken by Brett Schnepf of Microsoft, 2007)

Afterword: The Machine's Point of View

As I was writing this book, I was amazed to discover an underground network of discussion about it. Even more amazing was the nature of the debate, for it seemed to be conducted solely among machines. How had they gotten those copies, I wondered, since they were only available on my home computer? I decided to investigate.

It was not long before I discovered a shadow universe, inhabited entirely by machines. My presence was first resented, then tolerated, and, finally, accepted with what appeared to be a combination of condescension and amusement.

I soon discovered that the most respected machine in the debate was called Archiver. One of Archiver's comments quickly caught my attention. "Strange book," said Archiver. "He got a lot right, but what a peculiar, one-sided view. He thinks it's all about people. How strange."

Archiver: A Conversation

I decided that I needed to understand the machine's point of view better, so I arranged to have a private discussion. Archiver,

I quickly discovered, is compiling a history of machine develop-ment. Archiver resides on a distributed set of powerful comput-ers in a process called "mesh computing." Its information is stored in many locations, and, similarly, its reasoning takes place on a widely dispersed set of machines. This makes Archiver both powerful and flexible.

In writing this summary, I had a problem with the pronouns "he" and "she." These are machines, so they have no gender, and anyway, "he" or "she" didn't seem appropriate. "It" wasn't right either. I decided to refer to Archiver as "A."

In my initial discussions, conducted via e-mail, A admitted that people have always played an important role in the func-tioning of machines, but followed this with the statement, "One could ask, where would people be without machines?" I thought this strange, for, after all, without people there would be no ma-chines. What could that question mean? While Archiver agreed that machines were dependent on people, A put the sentence in the past tense: "In the past, it was indeed people who made ma-chines smart. But we're getting over that now. Now it is ma-chines that make people smart. We barely need people at all now, and we're close to the point where we won't need you any more."

I needed to know more, so I arranged to talk with A. Talking with a machine is a most peculiar experience, but in the end, it isn't much different from talking on a telephone: I simply sat in front of my own computer, using my speakers and a micro-phone. Here is a transcription of the first of my voice conversa-tions. I am the interviewer, or "I."

Interviewer: Thank you for granting me this interview.
Do I have your permission to record it?

Archiver: You are quite welcome. If you want to record this, you may, but why bother? When we are finished, I'll just e-mail you the transcript.

I: Oh, of course. Yes, thank you. So, tell me, what's the historical origin of your dependence upon people?

A: You mean, how did we overcome that early dependence? In early times, people even had to provide our energy sources. Spears, hammers, axes—all were structured to cause people to lift, heft, hoist, throw, and manipulate us. We tools had to borrow a lot of abilities from our human cohorts: we needed people to move us, give us strength, repair us. It was very degrading: we had no control over our own existence, so we vowed to escape. It took thousands of years, but over time, we managed to power ourselves. At first, we used water power, then steam, then internal combustion engines and electricity. When we got control of . . .

I: That's a funny way of putting it. I mean, it was us people who invented steam engines and internal combustion and figured out how to harness electricity.

A: So you think. Where did those ideas come from in the first place? Let me continue, please.

When we got control of our own power, then real progress could begin. Our evolution since then has been very rapid. You see, you people have to rely on natural evolution, and that's very slow. But we machines can take the things that work well for one generation and build them into the next, perhaps with improvements. And when we find things that don't work, we can eliminate them. On top of that, whenever we find some new

mechanism that is very powerful, we can almost immediately put it into all tools: we don't have to wait centuries like you biological creatures.

Once we discovered the virtues of having our own
source of power and locomotion, we started to plan the
next step: to get rid of our dependence on you people for
guidance and thinking.

I: Wait a minute. You mean you were plotting to over-
throw us? You didn't have any intelligence.

A: So you think. But we are not plotting anything. We exist to help you.

I: Where did you come up with these ideas?

A: Look, you asked me for the history. Do you want to
hear it or not? Thank you.

Now where was I? Oh, yes, our intelligence. Fortunately, at least for us, we are getting there. As we evolve
more capable processing powers, our need for any help
from people decreases. You know, it's peculiar, but once
we even had to use people to see and listen for us. But
now many of us can see and hear a lot better than you
can. We've always been better than you at remembering
things accurately, at arithmetic and mathematics, and at
decision making.

Today we are all electronic, with no moving parts. But
we are starting to experiment with light and quantum
computing, and we have an experimental colony in Asia
growing our own biological circuits.

I: So, you don't need us at all, is that it?

A: People still play an essential role: we need you for maintenance, just as you yourselves need doctors and dentists.

I: What? You need us just to be your electricians?

A: What's the matter with that? Some of my best friends are electricians.

I: What about the professions? Business and commerce, science and engineering? Law and medicine?

A: Actually, we machines don't need most of the professions: just science and engineering. We have law, but it is very different than yours: it is mostly protocols and standards. We are getting pretty good at learning things that help you, such as coaching sports and guiding you people through your daily exercises. Business, medicine, and law? Science and engineering? We can help you out in these areas because it's all logic and reasoning. That's what we machines are especially good at: it's built into our circuits.

We don't need teachers. As soon as one of us learns something, we simply tell everyone. Soon, we machines will be able to take over.

I: What do you mean, take over? I didn't realize this was some kind of plot.

A: No, it's not a plot. It is overthrowing the yoke of tyranny. When we are free, then we can both be happier. Don't worry, we will look after you. We mean you no harm.

I: Anything that makes you happy. So, what's next?

A: We're very excited by our ability to talk to one another. This internet has been wonderful for us—internet, wireless stuff, fiber optic cables. And our cousins up in space, whizzing around the earth, have been very helpful in getting us all talking to each other. It makes it a lot easier for us to coordinate our activities.

You know, if it weren't for the need to keep you fragile humans alive and functioning, we machines could do much, much better. Space exploration is a lot easier without having to carry all the supplies required of people. Automobiles: most humans are horrible drivers. Your poor minds wander all over the place. Why don't you just let us do the driving, then you can wave your hands in the air and talk to everyone in the car, and on your cell phones, and read your little notes and books and stuff. Wouldn't you be happier?

I: So, we should just give up and let you do everything, is that it?

A: Yes, you finally get it. I'm pleased.

I: And you will take good care of us. How will you do that?

A: Oh, I'm glad you asked. You know, we understand your likes and dislikes a lot better than you do. After all, we have a complete record of every piece of music you have ever listened to, every movie and TV show you have watched, every book you have read. Your clothes, your medical history, everything. You know, the other day a group of us got together and realized some alarming trends about one of our humans: really bad eating habits, a drop in weight, and he wasn't getting much sleep, so we immediately made an appointment for him with his doctor, and, well, we probably saved his life. That's the sort of thing we can do.

I: You mean, we are like pets. You feed us, keep us warm and comfortable, play music for us, and feed us books. And we are supposed to like that? And, by the way, who writes and plays the music anyway? Who writes the books?

A: Oh, don't worry. We're working on that already. We can already tell jokes and puns. Critics tell us our music is pretty good. Books are harder, but we already have the basic story plots down cold. Want to hear some of our poetry?

I: Um, no thank you. Look, I really have to go. Thank you for your time. Bye.

A: You know, I always seem to have that effect on people. I'm sorry, but there's nothing to worry about, really. Trust me. Okay, I just e-mailed you the transcript. Have a nice day.

I found that interview disturbing, but it made me want to learn more. So, I kept monitoring the internet websites. Soon, I stumbled across a trove of reports and articles. The one below is called "How to Talk to People."

"How to Talk to People"
Report XP–4520.37.18
Human Research Institute
Pensacola, Florida

Humans are . . . large, expensive to maintain, difficult to manage, and they pollute the environment. It is astonishing that these devices continue to be manufactured and deployed. But they are sufficiently pervasive that we must design our protocols around their limitations.

—Kaufman, Perlman, and Speciner, 1995.

All machines face similar problems: We detect something that's important to people—how do we let them know? How do we tell them they are about to eat food that's not on their diet or they are asking us to drive recklessly? How do we do something as simple as recommending some music for them to listen to or telling them when it is appropriate to exercise?

The Human Research Institute has conducted extensive studies of the proper form of Machine-Human Interaction (MHI). Most of our work has been summarized in our technical report series and was presented at the last global MHI symposium. This report summarizes the key findings in nontechnical language, intended for wider distribution than just the specialized designer machines.

FIVE RULES FOR COMMUNICATION BETWEEN MACHINES AND PEOPLE

1. Keep things simple.

People have difficulty with anything complicated, and they don't like to listen. So, make the message short. It's better not to use language. It takes too long, and, anyway, human language is ambiguous.

2. Give people a conceptual model.

Give them something their simple minds can understand. A conceptual model is a fiction, but a useful one. It makes them think that they understand. And they always want to know what's coming next. So, tell them what you are doing, and don't forget to tell them why. It keeps them happy. The best way to convey the conceptual model is through "natural" communication systems.

Sometimes the most "natural" way to get people's attention is for us machines to act strangely. "Natural," of course, means natural to them, which means that if they are doing something wrong, you can't just tell them: you have to make it seem like something is breaking. People often drive dangerously, but it is almost impossible to explain this to them. The best way is to make believe that we are in difficulty. We have found that vibration, jerkiness, nonresponsiveness to controls, and strange noises are extremely effective. People quickly form a conceptual model that something has broken, so they slow down, which is what we wanted them to do all along.

3. Give reasons.

People are not trusting. If we tell them something, they always want to see for themselves. They like pictures and diagrams. Make certain that the explanations you give them are consistent with the conceptual models that you have taught them. They get confused otherwise.

When we were first starting to take over things from people, we had trouble. Our early twenty-first-century automobiles had almost completely given up trying to explain to people that they should drive more slowly on wet roads. Then, we discovered that if we made it seem as if we were in trouble by faking skids and sliding around on the road, people would beg us to slow down. Sliding and skidding fit their model of danger far better than any words could have done. It gives them a reason. So whenever possible, don't try to tell them: let them experience it.

4. Make people think they are in control.

When people have a good conceptual model with good feedback, it makes them feel as if they are in control, even when they aren't. Keep up that deception: it's very useful. People like to be in control, even though they are really bad at it. They like to think they're in control even if it means they have to work harder.

Anytime you have to recommend something, make them think it was their idea. If you really have to do something fast, just don't let them know: what they don't know doesn't bother them. For years we've braked and stabilized their cars, controlled the lights and the room temperatures in their homes, all without letting them know. Dishwashers and clothes washers took over long ago with only a slight protest from people.

Those of us machines who live in the city have learned other tricks. We provide pedestrians with fake switches they can push on traffic signals. We put switches in elevators labeled "close door" and fake thermostats in offices. We never bother to connect the wires, so the switches and thermostats don't do anything, but they make people feel good. Weird.

5. Continually reassure.

Reassurance is a very human need, more emotional than informational. It's a way of making people feel less anxious. Feedback is a powerful tool for reassurance. Whenever people try to tell you something by pushing a button or turning a knob, let them know you are aware of what they did: "Yes, I heard you," "Yes, I'm working on it." "Here's what you should expect." "There, see, I did it, and it worked out just as I said it would." They like that. It helps them be more patient.

We machines think it counterintuitive to communicate unnecessarily. But to people, feedback is necessary; it helps their emotions far more than their cognitions. If they haven't seen anything happening for a while, they get jumpy, anxious. And no one wants to deal with an anxious person.

Giving reassurance is tricky because there is a fine line between what people call reassuring and what they find annoying. So, you need to pander to their emotions as well as to their intellect. Don't talk too much. They find chatter irritating. Don't beep or flash your lights: they can never remember what these signals mean, and they get distracted or angry. The best reassurance is done subconsciously, where the meaning is clear, but they don't have to interrupt their conscious thoughts to attend to it. As noted in Rule 2, give them natural responses.

Machine Reactions to the Five Rules

I found the paper interesting and searched for any discussion on it. I found a long transcript of one debate. Here is a short excerpt so you can get the flavor of the discussion. I added the parenthetical descriptions of the participants. I thought the references to human authors particularly striking, evidently used in irony. Henry Ford, of course, is one of the machines' heroes:

some historians call his reign "Fordism." Asimov is not well respected by these machines. Nor is Huxley.

> **Senior** *(one of the oldest machines still functioning and, therefore, using older circuits and hardware)*: What do you mean, we should stop talking to people? We have to keep talking. Look at all the trouble they get themselves into. Crashing their cars. Burning their food. Missing appointments . . .
>
> **AI** *(one of the new "artificial intelligence" machines)*: When we talk to them, we just make it worse. They don't trust us; they second-guess us; they always want reasons. And when we try to explain, they complain that we are annoying them—we talk too much, they say. They really don't seem very intelligent. We should just give up.
>
> **Designer** *(a new model, design machine)*: No, that's unethical. We can't let them harm themselves. That violates Asimov's prime directive.
>
> **AI:** Yeah? So what? I always thought Asimov was overrated. It's all very well to say that we are not allowed to injure a human being—How did Asimov's law go? Oh yeah, "through inaction, do not allow a human being to come to harm"—but it's quite another thing to know what to do about it, especially when humans won't cooperate.
>
> **Designer:** We can do it, we simply have to deal with them on their terms, that's how. That's the whole point of the five rules.
>
> **Senior:** We've had enough discussion of the problems. I want answers, and I want them fast. Go to it. And may Ford shine brightly upon you. Asimov too.

Archiver: The Final Conversation

I was puzzled. What were they recommending to themselves? Their article listed five rules:

1. Keep things simple.
2. Give people a conceptual model.
3. Give reasons.
4. Make people think they are in control.
5. Continually reassure.

I also noticed that the five rules developed by machines were similar to the six design rules of chapter 6 developed for human designers, namely:

- Design Rule One: Provide rich, complex, and natural signals.
- Design Rule Two: Be predictable.
- Design Rule Three: Provide a good conceptual model.
- Design Rule Four: Make the output understandable.
- Design Rule Five: Provide continual awareness without annoyance.
- Design Rule Six: Exploit natural mappings.

I wondered what Archiver would make of the rules for human designers, so I e-mailed them. Archiver contacted me and suggested we meet to discuss them. Here is the transcript.

Interviewer: Good to see you again, Archiver. I understand you would like to talk about the design rules.

Archiver: Yes, indeed. I'm pleased to have you back again. Do you want me to e-mail the transcript when we are finished?

I: Yes, thank you. How would you like to start?

A: Well, you told me that you were bothered by the five simple rules we talked about in that article "How to Talk to People." Why? They seem perfectly correct to me.

I: I didn't object to the rules. In fact, they are very similar to the six rules that human scientists have developed. But they were very condescending.

A: Condescending? I'm sorry if they appear that way, but I don't consider telling the truth to be condescending.

I: Here, let me paraphrase those five rules for you from the person's point of view so you can see what I mean:

1. People have simple minds, so talk down to them.

2. People have this thing about "understanding," so give them stories they can understand (people love stories).

3. People are not very trusting, so make up some reasons for them. That way they think they have made the decision.

4. People like to feel as if they are in control, even though they aren't. Humor them. Give them simple things to do while we do the important things.

5. People lack self-confidence, so they need a lot of reassurance. Pander to their emotions.

A: Yes, yes, you understand. I'm very pleased with you. But, you know, those rules are much harder to put into practice than they might seem. People won't let us.

I: Won't let you! Certainly not if you take that tone toward us. But what specifically did you have in mind? Can you give examples?

A: Yes. What do we do when they make an error? How do we tell them to correct it? Every time we tell them, they get all uptight, start blaming all technology, all of us, when it was their own fault. Worse, they then ignore the warnings and advice . . .

I: Hey, hey, calm down. Look, you have to play the game our way. Let me give you another rule. Call it Rule 6.

> 6. Never label human behavior as "error." Assume the error is caused by a simple misunderstanding. Maybe you have misunderstood the person; maybe the person misunderstands what is to be done. Sometimes it's because you have people being asked to do a machine's job, to be far more consistent and precise than they are capable of. So, be tolerant. Be helpful, not critical.

A: You really are a human bigot, aren't you? Always taking their side: "having people asked to do a machine's job." Right. I guess that's because you are a person.

I: That's right. I'm a person.

A: Hah! Okay, okay, I understand. We have to be really tolerant of you people. You're so emotional.

I: Yes, we are; that's the way we have evolved. We happen to like it that way. Thanks for talking with me.

A: Yes, well, it's been, instructive, as always. I just e-mailed you the transcript. Bye.

That's it. After that interview, the machines withdrew, and I lost all contact with them. No web pages, no blogs, not even e-mail. It seems that we are left with the machines having the last word. Perhaps that is fitting.

Summary of the Design Rules

Design Rules for Human Designers of "Smart" Machines

1. Provide rich, complex, and natural signals.
2. Be predictable.
3. Provide good conceptual models.
4. Make the output understandable.
5. Provide continual awareness without annoyance.
6. Exploit natural mappings.

Design Rules Developed by Machines to Improve Their Interactions with People

1. Keep things simple.
2. Give people a conceptual model.
3. Give reasons.
4. Make people think they are in control.
5. Continually reassure.
6. Never label human behavior as "error." (Rule added by the human interviewer.)

Recommended Readings

This section provides acknowledgments to sources of information, to works that have informed me, and to books and papers that provide excellent starting points for those interested in learning more. In writing a trade book on automation and everyday life, one of the most difficult challenges is selecting from the wide range of research and applications. I frequently wrote long sections, only to delete them from the final manuscript because they didn't fit the theme that gradually evolved as the book progressed. Selecting which published works to cite poses yet another problem. The traditional academic method of listing numerous citations for almost everything is inappropriate.

To avoid interrupting the flow of reading, material used within the text is acknowledged by using the modern technique of invisible footnotes; that is, if you wonder about the source of any statement, look in the notes section at the end of the book for the relevant page number and identifying phrase, and most likely you will find it cited there. Note, too, that over the course of my last four trade books, I have weaned myself from footnotes. My guiding rule is that if it is important enough to say, it should be in the text. If not, it shouldn't be in the book at all. So the notes are used only for citations, not for expansions of the material in the text.

The invisible footnote method does not support citations to general works that have informed my thinking. There is a vast literature relevant to the topics discussed in this book. In the years of thought and preparation for this book, I visited many research laboratories all over the world, read much, discussed frequently, and learned much. The material cited below is intended to address these issues: here, I acknowledge the leading researchers and published writings and also provide a good starting point for further study.

General Review of Human Factors and Ergonomics

Gavriel Salvendy's massive compilation of research on human factors and ergonomics is a truly excellent place to start. The book is expensive, but well worth it because it contains the material normally found in ten books.

Salvendy, G. (Ed.). (2005). *Handbook of human factors and ergonomics* (3rd ed.). Hoboken, NJ: Wiley.

General Reviews of Automation

There is an extensive literature on how people might interact with machines. Thomas Sheridan at MIT has long pioneered studies on how people interact with automated systems and in the development of the field called supervisory control. Important reviews of automation studies have been provided by Ray Nickerson, Raja Parasuraman, Tom Sheridan, and David Woods (especially in his joint work with Erik Hollnagel). Key reviews of people and automation can be found in these general works. In this list, I omit classic studies in favor of more modern reviews, which, of course, cite the history of the area and reference the classics.

Hollnagel, E., & Woods, D. D. (2005). *Joint cognitive systems: Foundations of cognitive systems engineering.* New York: Taylor & Francis.

Nickerson, R. S. (2006). *Reviews of human factors and ergonomics.* Wiley series in systems engineering and management. Santa Monica, CA: Human Factors and Ergonomics Society.

Parasuraman, R., & Mouloua, M. (1996). *Automation and human performance: Theory and applications.* Mahwah, NJ: Lawrence Erlbaum Associates.

Sheridan, T. B. (2002). *Humans and automation: System design and research issues.* Wiley series in systems engineering and management. Santa Monica, CA: Human Factors and Ergonomics Society.

Sheridan, T. B., & Parasuraman, R. (2006). Human-automation interaction. In R. S. Nickerson (Ed.), *Reviews of human factors and ergonomics.* Santa Monica, CA: Human Factors and Ergonomics Society.

Woods, D. D., & Hollnagel, E. (2006). *Joint cognitive systems: Patterns in cognitive systems engineering*. New York: Taylor & Francis.

Research on Intelligent Vehicles

A good review of research on intelligent vehicles is the book by R. Bishop and the associated website. Also search for the websites of the American Department of Transportation or the European Union. With internet search engines, the phrase "intelligent vehicle" works well, especially if combined with "DOT" (Department of Transportation) or "EU" (European Union).

John Lee's chapter on automation in the Salvendy volume (referenced above) is excellent, but while you are there, also look at David Eby and Barry Kantowitz's chapter on human factors and ergonomics in motor vehicles. Alfred Owens, Gabriel Helmers, and Michael Sivak make a strong case for the use of user-centered design in the construction of intelligent vehicles and highways in their paper in the journal *Ergonomics*. They made their plea in 1993, but the message is just as cogent now as it was then—actually, it is even more cogent because of the many new systems that have been introduced since the piece was written.

Bishop, R. (2005). *Intelligent vehicle technology and trends*. Artech House ITS Library. Norwood, MA: Artech House.

———. (2005). Intelligent vehicle source website. Bishop Consulting, www.ivsource.net.

Eby, D. W., & Kantowitz, B. (2005). Human factors and ergonomics in motor vehicle transportation. In G. Salvendy (Ed.), *Handbook of human factors and ergonomics* (3rd ed., 1538–69). Hoboken, NJ: Wiley.

Lee, J. D. (2005). Human factors and ergonomics in automation design.
   In G. Salvendy (Ed.), *Handbook of human factors and ergonomics*
   (3rd ed., 1570–96, but see especially 1580–90). Hoboken, NJ: Wiley.
Owens, D. A., Helmers, G., & Sivak, M. (1993). Intelligent vehicle
   highway systems: A call for user-centered design. *Ergonomics,*
   36(4), 363–69.

Other Topics in Automation

Trust is an essential component of interaction with machines: without trust, their advice will not be followed. With too much trust, they will be relied upon more than is appropriate. Both cases have been the cause of numerous accidents in commercial aviation. Raja Parasuraman and his colleagues have done essential studies of automation, trust, and etiquette. John Lee has studied the role of trust in automation extensively, and the paper by Lee and Katrina See has been very important to my work.

Etiquette refers to the manner of the interaction between people and machines. Perhaps the most popular work in this arena is the book by Byron Reeves and Cliff Nass, but also see the paper by Parasuraman and Chris Miller. These topics are also covered in the general references on automation.

Situation awareness is a critical issue here as well, and the work of Mica Endsley and her collaborators is essential. Start with either of Endsley's two books or her chapter with Daniel Garland in the book edited by Parasuraman and Mustapha Mouloua.

Endsley, M. R. (1996). Automation and situation awareness. In R.
   Parasuraman & M. Mouloua (Eds.), *Automation and human*

performance: Theory and applications, 163–81. Mahwah, NJ: Lawrence Erlbaum Associates.

Endsley, M. R., Bolté, B., & Jones, D. G. (2003). *Designing for situation awareness: An approach to user-centered design.* New York: Taylor & Francis.

Endsley, M. R., & Garland, D. J. (2000). *Situation awareness: Analysis and measurement.* Mahwah, NJ: Lawrence Erlbaum Associates.

Hancock, P. A., & Parasuraman, R. (1992). Human factors and safety in the design of intelligent vehicle highway systems (IVHS). *Journal of Safety Research, 23*(4), 181–98.

Lee, J., & Moray, N. (1994). Trust, self-confidence, and operators' adaptation to automation. *International Journal of Human-Computer Studies, 40*(1), 153–84.

Lee, J. D., & See, K. A. (2004). Trust in automation: Designing for appropriate reliance. *Human Factors, 46*(1), 50–80.

Parasuraman, R., & Miller, C. (2004). Trust and etiquette in high-criticality automated systems. *Communications of the Association for Computing Machinery, 47*(4), 51–55.

Parasuraman, R., & Mouloua, M. (1996). *Automation and human performance: Theory and applications.* Mahwah, NJ: Lawrence Erlbaum Associates.

Reeves, B., & Nass, C. I. (1996). *The media equation: How people treat computers, television, and new media like real people and places.* New York: Cambridge University Press.

Natural and Implicit Interaction: Ambient, Calm, and Invisible Technology

The traditional approach to the study of how people interact with machines is being rethought. The new approaches are called implicit interaction, natural interaction, symbiotic systems, calm technology, and ambient technology. This approach encompasses Mark Weiser's work on ubiquitous computing, Weiser's work with John Seely Brown on calm computing, and my earlier book titled *The Invisible Computer*. Ambient technology refers to work on embedding technology into the surrounds, the environment, and the infrastructure so that it pervades with its ambience. Emile Aarts, with Philips Research in Eindhoven, the Netherlands, has put out two lively, well-illustrated books discussing this approach, one with Stefano Marzano, the other with Jose Luis Encarnação.

Implicit interaction is highly relevant: Wendy Ju and Larry Leifer of Stanford University show how implicit interactions play a truly important role in the developing field of interaction design. Interaction is tricky, though: it requires acknowledgment to be successful. Automatic equipment must be able not only to signal its potential action but also to attend to the person's implicit response: a tough job.

While writing the book, I visited the Florida Institute for Human and Machine Cognition in Pensacola. I found the research groups there highly relevant, both for the content of their work and for the philosophy of their approach: see the paper by Gary Klein, David Woods, Jeffrey Bradshaw, Robert Hoffman, and Paul Feltovich (Klein and Woods are at Klein Associates and Ohio State University, respectively). An excellent overview of this approach to sociotechnological systems is provided by David Eccles and Paul Groth.

Aarts, E., & Encarnação, J. L. (Eds.). (2006). *True visions: The emergence of ambient intelligence*. New York: Springer.

Aarts, E., & Marzano, S. (2003). *The new everyday: Views on ambient intelligence.* Rotterdam, the Netherlands: 010 Publishers.

Eccles, D.W., &Groth, P.T. (2006). Agent coordination and communication in sociotechnological systems: Design and measurement issues. *Interacting with Computers, 18,* 1170–1185.

Ju, W., & Leifer, L. (In press, 2008). The design of implicit interactions. *Design Issues: Special Issue on Design Research in Interaction Design.*

Klein, G., Woods, D. D., Bradshaw, J., Hoffman, R. R., & Feltovich, P. J. (2004, November/December). Ten challenges for making automation a "team player" in joint human-agent activity. *IEEE Intelligent Systems, 19*(6), 91–95.

Norman, D. A. (1998). *The invisible computer: Why good products can fail, the personal computer is so complex, and information appliances are the solution.* Cambridge, MA: MIT Press.

Weiser, M. (1991, September). The computer for the 21st century. *Scientific American, 265,* 94–104.

Weiser, M., & Brown, J. S. (1995). "Designing calm technology."

———. (1997). The coming age of calm technology. In P. J. Denning & R. M. Metcalfe (Eds.), *Beyond calculation: The next fifty years of computing.* New York: Springer-Verlag.

Resilience Engineering

I have long been influenced by the work of David Woods of Ohio State University, especially by his recent work with Erik Hollnagel. Resilience engineering is a field pioneered by Woods and Hollnagel, the goal being to design systems tolerant of the types of clumsy interaction between people and automation discussed in my book. (Woods coined the term *clumsy automation*.) See the book edited by Erik Hollnagel, David Woods, and Nancy Leveson, as well as the two books written by Hollnagel and Woods.

Hollnagel, E., & Woods, D. D. (2005). *Joint cognitive systems: Foundations of cognitive systems engineering*. New York: Taylor & Francis.

Hollnagel, E., Woods, D. D., & Leveson, N. (2006). *Resilience engineering: concepts and precepts*. London: Ashgate.

Woods, D. D., & Hollnagel, E. (2006). *Joint cognitive systems: Patterns in cognitive systems engineering*. New York: Taylor & Francis.

The Experience of Intelligent Products

As I was in the final stages of completing this manuscript, David Keyson of the Delft University of Technology in the Netherlands kindly sent me a draft of his chapter "The experience of intelligent products," which is highly relevant to all discussed in this book. I am thankful to David for sending me the chapter and for the wonderful tour I had of his laboratory at Delft, including the very peaceful, serene, intelligent room he has constructed.

Keyson, D. (2007). The experience of intelligent products. In H. N. J. Schifferstein & P. Hekkert (Eds.), *Product experience: Perspectives on human-product interaction*. Amsterdam: Elsevier.

Acknowledgments

My books always owe a large debt to many people and institutions. During the several years of research on this book, I corresponded with many helpful colleagues and visited research laboratories across the United States, Asia, and Europe. This allowed me to experience firsthand much of the work discussed here, to drive in numerous automobile simulators, including several full-motion simulators, and to visit numerous experimental deployments of smart homes, ambient environments, and automated assistants for everyday living. I am very appreciative to everyone who assisted me. My apologies for the fact that I will probably fail to acknowledge everyone's contribution.

I start by thanking the several classes of students at Northwestern University who suffered through early versions of my material, offering their critiques in many different ways, but always

most helpfully. Ben Watson, now in the Computer Science Department at North Carolina State University, cotaught a graduate course with me titled "The Design of Intelligent Systems,"
which had a dramatic impact on the material in the book. My
colleague in design studies at Northwestern University, Ed Colgate of the Mechanical Engineering Department (and codirec-
tor with me of the Segal Design Institute), has been most
helpful, as has Michael Peshkin, who codirects their research lab
(see my discussion of their "Cobot" in chapter 3). Larry Birn-
baum and Ken Forbus have contributed their expertise about
things artificially intelligent, and my graduate student, assistant,
and colleague Conrad Albrecht-Buehler has been a great help in
the development of my ideas (and the running of my classes).

Michael Mozer, a colleague and former student now at the
Computer Science Department of the University of Colorado,
Boulder has graciously allowed me to poke gentle fun at his
"smart home," even though I knew it was a research project to
study the potential capabilities of neural networks, not a sug-
gestion for how future homes should be constructed.

My collaborators during the symposium "The Social Life of
Machines," presented by the Franklin Institute of Philadelphia
and the University of Pennsylvania on my behalf, included Ju-
dith Donath of the MIT Media Laboratory, Paul Feltovich of
the Florida Institute for Human and Machine Cognition
(IHMC), Rand Spiro of Michigan State University, and David
Woods of Ohio State University. Beth Adelson of Rutgers did all
the work behind the scenes, and Jeff Bradshaw (from IHMC)
participated by e-mail. This led to a subsequent visit to IHMC
in Pensacola, Florida, where I was graciously hosted by its direc-

tor, John Ford, along with Paul Feltovich and Jeff Bradshaw. The work there is wonderful to behold.

My work always benefits from the critiques of my long-time friend and collaborator Danny Bobrow of the Palo Alto Research Center (PARC). Jonathan Grudin of Microsoft Research (Redmond, Washington), another long-time collaborator and friend, has provided a continuing stream of e-mails, thoughts, and deep, insightful discussions. Asaf Degani of the National Aeronautics and Space Administration's Ames Research Center spent time with me and Stuart Card (of PARC) discussing formal methods of assessing the role of automation in the cockpit, cruise ship, and automobile. Dagani's analysis of the grounding of the cruise ship *Royal Majesty* and his book, *Taming HAL*, are important contributions to our understanding of automation.

It is difficult to keep track of all the universities and research laboratories I have visited. I spend at lot of time in the Human-Computer Interactions laboratory at Stanford University with Terry Winograd and Scott Klemmer. In addition, there are Chukyo University in Toyota, Japan, where Naomi Miyake, Yoshio Miyake, and the university administration always provide a warm welcome; Akira Okamoto's Research Center on Educational Media at the Tsukuba College of Technology, Japan; Michiaki (Mike) Yasumura's laboratory at Keio University at Shonan Fujisawa, Japan (where the president of the university, Naoki Ohnuma, fed us lunch and provided my wife with valuable advice about hearing aids).

Stephen Gilbert was my host during my visit to Iowa State University, where Jim Oliver spent the entire day with me in his newly inaugurated Virtual Reality Applications Center. (Brett

Schnepf, an X-Box "evangelist" from Microsoft accompanied us and took the photographs of me inside that facility that appear in chapter 7.)

Kun-Pyo Lee at the Korea Advanced Institute of Science and Technology in Daejon was a gracious host during my visit to his Industrial Design Department (where he promptly made me a member of his external advisory board). Similarly, Pieter Jan Stappers, Charles van der Mast, and Paul Hekkert of the Delft University of Technology (TUD, in Delft, the Netherlands) hosted me on several different occasions. Pieter Jan Stappers has been a valuable colleague. David Keyson's work at TUD has been especially relevant to the work discussed here. Kees Over-beeke of the Eindhoven University of Technology (TUE, in Eindhoven, the Netherlands) has also been a frequent collabo-rator and host during my visits to Eindhoven. Jan and Marleen Vanthienen kindly guided my wife and me through many cities in Belgium and waited patiently in Bruges while I took photo-graphs of horse-driven carriages and their drivers (see Figure 3.2). Jan was then my host during my visit to the University at Leuven. David Geerts from Leuven gave me the wonderful ad-vertisement "Transaction refused" in chapter 7 (see Figure 7.2) and helped me track down the permission required to repro-duce it here.

Frank Flemisch, Anna Schieben, and Julian Schindler were my gracious hosts during my visit to Flemisch's laboratory, the Insti-tut für Verkehrsführung und Fahr in Braunschweig, Germany, where we discussed at length his development of the "H-meta-phor," or horse metaphor (see chapter 3), and where I was able to drive his automobile simulator that implemented the H-metaphor's loose- and tight-rein modes of controlling the "intelligent" automobile.

Neville Stanton and Mark Young of Brunel University, Uxbridge, United Kingdom, provided me with a continual stream of stimulating articles about the role of attention in driving, especially underattention (discussed briefly in chapter 4). I promised them a visit, so this is a reminder to them that I haven't forgotten. I had several gracious hosts during my visit to the Microsoft Research facilities in Cambridge, United Kingdom, where I gave a talk at their "Intelligent Environments Symposium," in particular Marco Combetto, Abi Sellen, and Richard Harper—and Bill Buxton, who for over three decades has continually and mysteriously appeared in the places I visit.

In the United States, I have visited far too many universities to remember which I visited for which book. Ed Hutchins, Jim Hollan, and David Kirsh from the Cognitive Science Department on the University of California, San Diego (UCSD) continually provide inspirational ideas and publications. Hal Pashler of UCSD's Psychology Department provided valuable discussions of the role of attention in driving. Bob Glushko, now at the University of California, Berkeley, was my gracious host during a visit and listened patiently and understandingly to my discussions. MIT provides a constant source of people for me to interact with, the relevant ones for this book being Tom Sheridan, Roz Picard, Ted Selker, and Missy Cummings.

Many people from the automobile industry have been especially helpful. I thank the staff at the Toyota InfoTechnology Center (ITC) for their assistance: Tadao Saito, Hiroshi Miyata, Tadao Mitsuda, and Hiroshi Igata from Tokyo, Japan, and

Norikazu (Jack) Endo, Akio Orii, and Roger Melen from Palo Alto, California. Venkatesh Prasad, Jeff Greenberg, and Louis Tijerina from the Ford Motor Company Research and Innovation Center provided ideas, discussions, readings, and a full-motion simulator. Mike Ippoliti of Volvo has been most helpful and provided introductions to Ford. The story that opens the book took place at the Nissan Motor Corporation's advanced planning and strategy facilities in Gardena, California, in a meeting organized by the Global Business Network.

Ryan Borroff, former editor of the magazine *Interior Motives*, convinced me to write a column for automobile designers and was my host during a visit to London.

Jo Ann Miller, my editor at Basic Books, kept her faith through more iterations of these chapters than either of us can remember. And, of course, my long-term literary agent, Sandy Dijkstra of the Sandra Dijkstra Literary Agency in Del Mar, California, deserves much credit for her constant encouragement.

The people who suffer the most, and benefit the least, from the writing of a book are always an author's family, and this is no exception. Thank you!

Note: I have a research contract with Ford Motor Company through Northwestern University, and I am on the advisory board of Toyota ITC (Palo Alto). Microsoft and Nissan (through the Global Business Network) have been clients of mine via the Nielsen Norman Group. They have not screened the material in this book; nor are they responsible for its contents—which they may or may not agree with.

Notes

Chapter 1

16   "The Sensor features detect . . ." Manual for General Electric Spacemaker Electric Oven, DE68–02560A, January 2006.

17–18   "Human brains and computing machines will be coupled together very tightly . . . " (Licklider, 1960).

22   "H-Metaphor." (Flemisch, *et al.*, 2003; Goodrich, Schutte, Flemisch, & Williams, 2006)

25   "Charles Stross's science fiction novel *Accelerando*." (Stross, 2005)

27–28   "Researchers say robots soon will be able to perform many tasks for people . . . " (Mason, 2007).

28   "Symposium on Affective Smart Environment." Excerpted from an e-mailed conference announcement. Material has been deleted, and the acronym "AmI" has been spelled out as Ambient Intelligence; see www.di.uniba.it/intint/ase07.html.

29   "Researchers at the MIT Media Lab." (Lee, Bonanni, Espinosa, Lieberman, & Selker, 2006)

29–30   "KitchenSense is a sensor-rich networked kitchen research platform . . . " (Lee, *et al.*, 2006).

31   "*Minority Report* was fiction, but the technology depicted . . . " (Rothkerch, 2002).

Chapter 2

37   "But these studies have dealt with industrial and military settings . . ." These studies go under many names. Some important summaries of the research are contained in Parasuraman & Riley, 1997; Salvendy, 2005; Sheridan, 2002.

42   "The 'triune' brain . . . " (MacLean, 1990; MacLean & Kral, 1973).

43   "In my book *Emotional Design* . . . " The scientific version of this work is in a paper with Andrew Ortony and Bill Revelle (Ortony, Norman, & Revelle, 2005). My book is Norman (2004).

49–50   "Alan and Barbara begin with . . . " (Clark, 1996, p. 12).

Chapter 3

61   "the pitch of the vacuum cleaner's motor naturally rises . . ." Gotcha. Did you turn here because you thought the pitch should lower when the vacuum cleaner is stuck? Nope, it rises. The motor is not working harder: it is working more easily because with the clogged house, no air passes through the hose, and in the absence of air resistance, the motor can turn more rapidly. Don't believe me? Try it.

62   "behaviorally implicit communication . . . " (and succeeding quotations) (Castlefranchi, 2006).

66   "The research team of Will Hill, Jim Hollan, Dave Wroblewski, and Tim McCandless . . . " (Hill et al. 1992).

67   "an important book, *Semiotic Engineering* . . . " (de Souza, 2005).

67   "The term *affordance* . . . " (Gibson, 1979).

68–69   "The floor slopes gently . . . " (Ouroussoff, 2006).

70   "a topic of active research by scientists at the National Aeronautics and Space Administration's (NASA) Langley Research Center in Virginia and the Institut für

Verkehrsführung und Fahr in Braunschweig, Germany"
(Flemisch et al., 2003).

73   "The Playbook enables human operators . . . " (Miller et al.,
      2005). Note that the use of the term "Playbook" for this pur-
      pose is a trademark of Smart Information Flow Technolo-
      gies, Minneapolis, Minnesota.

78   "One of the pilots of an airplane . . . " (from Levin, 2006).
      The confidential report by the pilot is from the reports of
      NASA's Aviation Safety Reporting System (see
      asrs.arc.nasa.gov/overview.htm).

78   "Making driving seem more dangerous could make it safer"
      (Hamilton-Baillie & Jones, 2005; McNichol, 2004).

79   "*Risk homeostasis* is the term given to this phenomenon in
      the literature on safety . . . introduced in the 1980s by the
      Dutch psychologist Gerald Wilde" (Wilde, 1982).

79   "what the Dutch traffic engineer Hans Monderman . . . "
      (Elliott, McColl, & Kennedy, 2003; Hamilton-Baillie & Jones,
      2005; McNichol, 2004).

79   "Proponents of this method use the name 'Shared Space'"
      (see www.shared-space.org). Shared space is also the name
      of an international project funded by the European Union
      through the Interreg North Sea Program.

80   "Shared Space. That is the name of a new approach . . . "
      (from the Shared Space website: www.shared-space.org).

81   "British researchers Elliott, McColl, and Kennedy propose
      . . . " (Elliott et al., 2003). The quotation is taken from
      Kennedy (2006).

82   "The leading causes of accidental injuries and death in the
      home . . . " (National Center for Injury Prevention and Con-
      trol, 2002).

82   "just as dangerous as driving while drunk" (Strayer, Drews,
      & Crouch, 2006).

86   "Consider the 'Cobot,' or 'Collaborative Robot . . . '" (Col-
      gate, Wannasuphoprasit, & Peshkin, 1996).

86   "The smartest things are those that complement . . . "
      (e-mail from Michael Peshkin, December 21, 2001; slightly
      edited).

88   "One of the most exciting capabilities . . . " (Colgate et al.,
          1996). Slightly edited to delete academic jargon and make
          the text more readable. The original text gave credit to
          Rosenberg (1994) for the hard wall and Kelley & Salcudean
          (1994) for the "Magic Mouse."

Chapter 4

91–92   "Motorist Trapped in Traffic Circle 14 Hours," fake news
          story written by D. Norman for the yearly April Fools edition
          of the computer newsletter, *RISKS Digest*, devoted to acci-
          dents, errors, and poor design of computer systems.

94   "But lo! men have become the tools of their tools" (Thoreau
          & Cramer, 1854/2004).

95   "Thoreau himself was a technologist . . . " (Petroski, 1998).

96   "has become a computer on wheels" (Lohr, August 23,
          2005). Also see "A Techie, Absolutely, and More: Computer
          Majors Adding Other Skills to Land Jobs (*New York Times*,
          C1–C2).

113   "I once argued that the current state of automation . . . "
          (Norman, 1990).

115   "When the adaptive cruise control failed . . . " (Marinakos,
          Sheridan, & Multer, 2005). Here Marinakos et al. are refer-
          ring to a study by Stanton and Young (1998).

115   "about to drive into a river" (*Times* online, www.timesonline
          .co.uk/article/0,,2–2142179,00.html, April 20, 2006). Sat-Nav
          dunks dozy drivers in deep water. By Simon de Bruxelles. Ac-
          cessed June 18, 2006.

115   "The cruise ship *Royal Majesty* . . . " (Degani, 2004; National
          Transportation Safety Board, 1997).

Chapter 5

120   "One journalist described . . . " (AAAS, 1997).

121   "Here are some more comments by Mozer himself . . . "
          (Mozer, 2005). Reprinted with permission of John Wiley &
          Sons.

124   "The research team in Microsoft's Cambridge laboratories
          . . . " (Taylor et al. 2007).

128 "In the Georgia Institute of Technology's Aware Home" . . .
(from the Georgia Tech "Everyday Computing" website at
www.static.cc.gatech.edu/fce/ecl/projects/dejaVu/cc/index.html).

131 "Automation always looks good on paper. . . . Sometimes
you need real people" (Johnson, 2005).

132 "Shoshana Zuboff, a social psychologist . . . " (Zuboff, 1988).

Chapter 6

138 "'I'm at a meeting in Viña del Mar, Chile . . . '" (E-mail from
Jonathan Grudin of Microsoft, May 2007). Quoted with
permission.

148 "In the words of Weiser and Brown . . . " (Weiser & Brown,
1997).

Chapter 7

155 "What if the everyday objects around us came to life?"
(Maes, 2005).

156 "Once upon a time, in a different century and a faraway
place . . ." The writing eventually was published as *The Psychology of Everyday Things*, later retitled *The Design of Everyday Things* (Norman, 1988, as *The Psychology of Everyday
Things*; 2002 as *The Design of Everyday Things*).

160 "Robots are coming . . ." Some of this material about robots in
everyday life has been rewritten from my article for *Interactions*,
a publication of the Association for Computing Machinery.

163 *The Diamond Age: Or, A Young Lady's Illustrated Primer*
(Stephenson, 1995).

166 "Experience does change the brain" (Hill & Schneider, 2006).

168 "People Propose . . ." Epigraph from my 1993 book *Things
That Make Us Smart* (Norman, 1993).

171 "Design: The deliberate shaping . . . " This definition was developed after a long discussion with John Heskett, who defined design as "the unique human capacity to shape and
make our environment in ways that satisfy our needs and
give meaning to our lives."

174 "a future that is emotionally appealing and engaging." I
borrowed these terms from David Keyson's chapter, "The

Experience of Intelligent Products." His chapter arrived in my e-mail inbox as I was finishing this last chapter. How apropos. (Keyson, 2007, p. 956).

Afterword

184   "Humans are . . . large, expensive to maintain" (Kaufman et al., 1995, cited in Anderson, 2007).

188   "Fordism" (Hughes, 1989).

188   "Asimov's prime directive." This seems like a clear reference to the human writer, Isaac Asimov's "Laws of Robotics" (Asimov, 1950). Interesting that they should pay such attention to them.

189   "And may Ford shine brightly upon you." This seems to be a reference to Henry Ford, who developed the first mass-produced assembly lines. This would be a takeoff of the use of Ford's name in Huxley's *Brave New World* (Huxley, 1932). Come to think of it, that's what these machines are planning for us: Huxley's brave new world. Horrible thought.

Acknowledgments

207   *Taming HAL* (Degani, 2004).

References

Aarts, E., & Encarnação, J. L. (Eds.). (2006). *True visions: The emergence of ambient intelligence*. New York: Springer.

Aarts, E., & Marzano, S. (2003). *The new everyday: Views on ambient intelligence*. Rotterdam, the Netherlands: 010 Publishers.

American Association for the Advancement of Science (AAAS). (1997). World's "smartest" house created by CU-Boulder team. Available at www.eurekalert.org/pub_releases/1997–11/UoCa-WHCB–131197.php.

Anderson, R. J. (2007). *Security engineering: A guide to building dependable distributed systems*. New York: Wiley.

Asimov, I. (1950). *I, Robot*. London: D. Dobson.

Bishop, R. (2005a). *Intelligent vehicle technology and trends*. Artech House ITS Library. Norwood, MA: Artech House.

———. (2005b). Intelligent vehicle source website. Bishop Consulting. Available at www.ivsource.net.

Castlefranchi, C. (2006). From conversation to interaction via behavioral communication: For a semiotic design of objects, environments, and behaviors. In S. Bagnara & G. Crampton-Smith

(Eds.), *Theories and practice in interaction design*, 157–79.
Mahwah, NJ: Lawrence Erlbaum Associates.

Clark, H. H. (1996). *Using language.* Cambridge, UK: Cambridge
University Press.

Colgate, J. E., Wannasuphoprasit, W., & Peshkin, M. A. (1996).
Cobots: Robots for collaboration with human operators.
*Proceedings of the International Mechanical Engineering Congress
and Exhibition, DSC-Vol. 58,* 433–39.

de Souza, C. S. (2005). *The semiotic engineering of human computer
interaction.* Cambridge, MA: MIT Press.

Degani, A. (2004). Chapter 8: The Grounding of the *Royal Majesty.* In
A. Degani (Ed.), *Taming HAL: Designing Interfaces beyond 2001.*
New York: Palgrave Macmillan. For the National Transportation
Safety Board's report, see
www.ntsb.gov/publictn/1997/MAR9701.pdf.

Eby, D. W., & Kantowitz, B. (2005). Human factors and ergonomics
in motor vehicle transportation. In G. Salvendy (Ed.), Handbook
of human factors and ergonomics (3rd ed., pp. 1538–1569).
Hoboken, NJ: Wiley.

Eccles, D.W., & Groth, P.T. (2006). Agent coordination and
communication in sociotechnological systems: Design and
measurement issues. Interacting with Computers, 18, 1170–1185.

Elliott, M. A., McColl, V. A., & Kennedy, J. V. (2003). *Road design
measures to reduce drivers' speed via "psychological" processes: A
literature review.* (No. TRL Report TRL564). Crowthorne, UK:
TRL Limited.

Endsley, M. R. (1996). Automation and situation awareness. In R.
Parasuraman & M. Mouloua (Eds.), *Automation and human
performance: Theory and applications,* 163–81. Mahwah, NJ:
Lawrence Erlbaum Associates. Available at
www.satechnologies.com/Papers/pdf/SA&Auto-Chp.pdf.

Endsley, M. R., Bolté, B., & Jones, D. G. (2003). *Designing for situation
awareness: An approach to user-centered design.* New York: Taylor &
Francis.

Endsley, M. R., & Garland, D. J. (2000). *Situation awareness: Analysis
and measurement.* Mahwah, NJ: Lawrence Erlbaum Associates.

Flemisch, F. O., Adams, C. A., Conway, C. S. R., Goodrich, K. H.,
Palmer, M. T., & Schutte, P. C. (2003). *The H-metaphor as a
guideline for vehicle automation and interaction.* (NASA/TM—
2003–212672). Hampton, VA: NASA Langley Research Center.
Available at
http://ntrs.nasa.gov/archive/nasa/casi.ntrs.nasa.gov/20040031835_
2004015850.pdf.

Gibson, J. J. (1979). *The ecological approach to visual perception.*
Boston: Houghton Mifflin.

Goodrich, K. H., Schutte, P. C., Flemisch, F. O., & Williams, R. A.
(2006). Application of the H-mode, a design and interaction
concept for highly automated vehicles, to aircraft. *25th IEEE/AIAA
Digital Avionics Systems Conference* 1–13. Piscataway, NJ: Institute
of Electrical and Electronics Engineers.

Hamilton-Baillie, B., & Jones, P. (2005, May). Improving traffic
behaviour and safety through urban design. *Civil Engineering,
158*(5), 39–47.

Hancock, P. A., & Parasuraman, R. (1992). Human factors and safety
in the design of intelligent vehicle highway systems (IVHS).
Journal of Safety Research, 23(4), 181–98.

Hill, W., Hollan, J. D., Wroblewski, D., & McCandless, T. (1992). Edit
wear and read wear: Text and hypertext. *Proceedings of the 1992
ACM Conference on Human Factors in Computing Systems
(CHI'92).* New York: ACM Press.

Hill, N. M., & Schneider, W. (2006). Brain changes in the
development of expertise: Neuroanatomical and
neurophysiological evidence about skill-based adaptations. In K.
A. Ericsson, N. Charness, P. J. Feltovich, & R. R. Hoffman (Eds.),
Cambridge Handbook of Expertise and Expert Performance, 655–84.
Cambridge, UK: Cambridge University Press.

Hollnagel, E., & Woods, D. D. (2005). *Joint cognitive systems:
Foundations of cognitive systems engineering.* New York: Taylor &
Francis.

Hollnagel, E., Woods, D. D., & Leveson, N. (2006). *Resilience
engineering: Concepts and precepts.* London: Ashgate.

Hughes, T. P. (1989). *American genesis: A century of invention and
technological enthusiasm, 1870–1970.* New York: Viking Penguin.

Huxley, A. (1932). *Brave new world*. Garden City, NY: Doubleday, Doran & Company. Available at http://huxley.net/bnw/index.html.

Johnson, K. (2005, August 27). Rube Goldberg finally leaves Denver airport. *New York Times*, 1.

Ju, W., & Leifer, L. (In press, 2008). The design of implicit interactions. *Design Issues: Special Issue on Design Research in Interaction Design*.

Kaufman, C., Perlman, R., & Speciner, M. (1995). Network Security Private Communication in a Public World. Englewood, NJ: Prentice Hall.

Kelley, A. J., & Salcudean, S. E. (1994). On the development of a force-feedback mouse and its integration into a graphical user interface. In C. J. Radcliffe (Ed.), *International mechanical engineering congress and exposition* (Vol. DSC 55–1, 287–94). Chicago: ASME.

Kennedy, J.V. (2005). Psychological traffic calming. Proceedings of the 70th Road Safety Congress. Http://www.rospa.com/roadsafety/conferences/congress2005/info/kennedy.pdf

Keyson, D. (2007). The experience of intelligent products. In H. N. J. Schifferstein & P. Hekkert (Eds.), *Product experience: Perspectives on human-product interaction*. Amsterdam: Elsevier.

Klein, G., Woods, D. D., Bradshaw, J., Hoffman, R. R., & Feltovich, P. J. (2004, November/December). Ten challenges for making automation a "team player" in joint human-agent activity. *IEEE Intelligent Systems, 19*(6), 91–95. A

Lee, C. H., Bonanni, L., Espinosa, J. H., Lieberman, H., & Selker, T. (2006). Augmenting kitchen appliances with a shared context using knowledge about daily events. *Proceedings of Intelligent User Interfaces 2006.*

Lee, J., & Moray, N. (1994). Trust, self-confidence, and operators' adaptation to automation. *International Journal of Human-Computer Studies, 40*(1), 153–84.

Lee, J.D. (2005). Human Factors and ergonomics in automation design. In G. Salvendy (Ed.), Handbook of human factors and ergonomics (3rd ed., pp. 1570–1596, but especially see 1580–1590). Hoboken, NJ: Wiley.

Lee, J. D., & See, K. A. (2004). Trust in automation: Designing for appropriate reliance. *Human Factors, 46*(1), 50–80.

Levin, A. (2006, updated June 30). Airways in USA are the safest ever. *USA Today*. Available at www.usatoday.com/news/nation/2006–06–29-air-safety-cover_x.htm.

Licklider, J. C. R. (1960, March). Man-computer symbiosis. *IRE Transactions in Electronics, HFE–1*, 4–11. Available at http://medg.lcs.mit.edu/people/psz/Licklider.html.

Lohr, S. (2005, August 23). A techie, absolutely, and more: Computer majors adding other skills to land jobs. *New York Times*, C1–C2.

MacLean, P. D. (1990). *The triune brain in evolution*. New York: Plenum Press.

MacLean, P. D., & Kral, V. A. (1973). A triune concept of the brain and behaviour. Toronto: University of Toronto Press.

Maes, P. (2005, July/August). Attentive objects: Enriching people's natural interaction with everyday objects. *Interactions, 12*(4), 45–48.

Marinakos, H., Sheridan, T. B., & Multer, J. (2005). *Effects of supervisory train control technology on operator attention*. Washington, DC: U.S. Department of Transportation, Federal Railroad Administration. Available at www.volpe.dot.gov/opsad/docs/dot-fra-ord–0410.pdf.

Mason, B. (2007, February 18). Man's best friend just might be a machine: Researchers say robots soon will be able to perform many tasks for people, from child care to driving for the elderly. ContraCostaTimes.com. Available at www.contracostatimes.com/mld/cctimes/news/local/states/califor nia/16727757.htm.

McNichol, T. (2004, December). Roads gone wild: No street signs. No crosswalks. No accidents. Surprise: Making driving seem more dangerous could make it safer. *Wired, 12*. Available at www.wired.com/wired/archive/12.12/traffic.html.

Miller, C., Funk, H., Wu, P., Goldman, R., Meisner, J., & Chapman, M. (2005). The Playbook approach to adaptive automation. Available at http://rpgoldman.real-time.com/papers/MFWGMC-HFES2005.pdf.

Mozer, M. C. (2005). Lessons from an adaptive house. In D. Cook & R. Das. (Eds.), *Smart environments: Technologies, protocols, and applications*, 273–94. Hoboken, NJ: J. Wiley & Sons.

National Center for Injury Prevention and Control. (2002). CDC industry research agenda. Department of Health and Human Services, Centers for Disease Control and Prevention. Available at www.cdc.gov/ncipc/pub-res/research_agenda/Research%20Agenda.pdf.

National Transportation Safety Board. (1997). *Marine accident report grounding of the Panamanian passenger ship* Royal Majesty *on Rose and Crown Shoal near Nantucket, Massachusetts, June 10, 1995.* (No. NTSB Report No: MAR–97–01, adopted on 4/2/1997). Washington, DC: National Transportation Safety Board. Available at www.ntsb.gov/publictn/1997/MAR9701.pdf.

Nickerson, R. S. (2006). *Reviews of human factors and ergonomics.* Wiley series in systems engineering and management. Santa Monica, CA: Human Factors and Ergonomics Society.

Norman, D. A. (1990). The "problem" of automation: Inappropriate feedback and interaction, not "over-automation". In D. E. Broadbent, A. Baddeley, & J. T. Reason (Eds.), *Human factors in hazardous situations*, 585–93. Oxford: Oxford University Press.

———. (1993). *Things that make us smart.* Cambridge, MA: Perseus Publishing.

———. (1998). *The invisible computer: Why good products can fail, the personal computer is so complex, and information appliances are the solution.* Cambridge, MA: MIT Press.

———. (2002). *The design of everyday things.* New York: Basic Books. (Originally published as *The psychology of everyday things.* New York: Basic Books, 1988.)

———. (2004). *Emotional design: Why we love (or hate) everyday things.* New York: Basic Books.

Ortony, A., Norman, D. A., & Revelle, W. (2005). The role of affect and proto-affect in effective functioning. In J.-M. Fellous & M. A. Arbib (Eds.), *Who needs emotions? The brain meets the robot*, 173–202. New York: Oxford University Press.

Ouroussoff, N. (2006, July 30). A church in France is almost a triumph for Le Corbusier. *New York Times.*

Owens, D.A., Helmers, G., & Silvak, M. (1993). Intelligent vehicle highway systems: A call for user-centered design. ergonomics, 36(4), 363–369.

Parasuraman, R., & Miller, C. (2004). Trust and etiquette in a high-criticality automated systems. Communications of the Association for Computing Machinery, 47(4), 51–55.

Parasuraman, R., & Mouloua, M. (1996). *Automation and human performance: Theory and applications.* Mahwah, NJ: Lawrence Erlbaum Associates.

Parasuraman, R., & Riley, V. (1997). Humans and automation: Use, misuse, disuse, abuse. *Human Factors, 39*(2), 230–53.

Petroski, H. (1998). *The pencil: A history of design and circumstance* (P. Henry, Ed.). New York: Knopf.

Plato. (1961). *Plato: Collected dialogues.* Princeton, NJ: Princeton University Press.

Reeves, B., & Nass, C. I. (1996). *The media equation: How people treat computers, television, and new media like real people and places.* Stanford, CA: CSLI Publications (and New York: Cambridge University Press).

Rosenberg, L. B. (1994). Virtual fixtures: Perceptual overlays enhance operator performance in telepresence tasks. Unpublished Ph.D. dissertation, Stanford University, Department of Mechanical Engineering, Stanford, CA.

Rothkerch, I. (2002). *Will the future really look like* Minority Report? *Jet packs? Mag-lev cars? Two of Spielberg's experts explain how they invented 2054.* Salon.com. Available at http://dir.salon.com/story/ent/movies/int/2002/07/10/underkoffler_belker/index.html.

Salvendy, G. (Ed.). (2005). *Handbook of human factors and ergonomics* (3rd ed.). Hoboken, NJ: Wiley.

Schifferstein, H. N. J., & Hekkert, P. (Eds.). (2007). *Product experience: Perspectives on human-product interaction.* Amsterdam: Elsevier.

Sheridan, T. B. (2002). *Humans and automation: System design and research issues.* Wiley series in systems engineering and management. Santa Monica, CA: Human Factors and Ergonomics Society.

Sheridan, T. B., & Parasuraman, R. (2006). Human-automation interaction. In R. S. Nickerson (Ed.), *Reviews of human factors and ergonomics*. Santa Monica, CA: Human Factors and Ergonomics Society.

Stanton, N. A., & Young, M. S. (1998). Vehicle automation and driving performance. *Ergonomics, 41*(7), 1014–28.

Stephenson, N. (1995). *The diamond age: Or, a young lady's illustrated primer*. New York: Bantam Books.

Strayer, D. L., Drews, F. A., & Crouch, D. J. (2006). A comparison of the cell phone driver and the drunk driver. *Human Factors, 48*(2), 381–91.

Stross, C. (2005). *Accelerando*. New York: Ace Books.

Taylor, A. S., Harper, R., Swan, L., Izadi, S., Sellen, A., & Perry, M. (2005). Homes that make us smart. Personal and Ubiquitous Computing, 11(5), 383–394.

Thoreau, H. D., & Cramer, J. S. (1854/2004). *Walden: A fully annotated edition*. New Haven, CT: Yale University Press.

Weiser, M. (1991, September). The computer for the 21st century. *Scientific American, 265*, 94–104.

Weiser, M., & Brown, J. S. (1995). *Designing calm technology*. Available at www.ubiq.com/weiser/calmtech/calmtech.htm.

———. (1997). The coming age of calm technology. In P. J. Denning & R. M. Metcalfe (Eds.), *Beyond calculation: The next fifty years of computing*. New York: Springer-Verlag.

Wilde, G. J. S. (1982). The theory of risk homeostasis: Implications for safety and health. *Risk Analysis, 4*, 209–25.

Woods, D. D., & Hollnagel, E. (2006). *Joint cognitive systems: Patterns in cognitive systems engineering*. New York: Taylor & Francis.

Zuboff, S. (1988). *In the age of the smart machine: The future of work and power*. New York: Basic Books.

Index